Listening to the Animals

FAMOUS ANIMALS

EDITED BY PHYLLIS HOBE

A GUIDEPOSTS BOOK

ACKNOWLEDGMENTS

Every attempt has been made to credit the sources of copyrighted material used in this book. If any such acknowledgment has been inadvertently omitted or miscredited, receipt of such information would be appreciated.

"A Medal for Tang" and "A Race With Death" are from *Dog Heroes,* by Tim Jones. Copyright © 1995 Tim Jones. Published by Epicenter Press.

"Beyond Appearances" and "The Bravest Cat in the World" are from *Hero Cats,* by Eric Swanson. Copyright © 1998 by Eric Swanson. Published by Andrews McMeel Publishing.

"Sergeant Stubby," by Mary Thurston, is from *PETS: Part of the Family,* May/June 2000.

"Boo's Challenge," by Kent and Donna Dannen, is used by permission of the authors.

"Piglet and Richard," "The Earthquake Dog" and "Simo: The Healing Dolphin" are from *Animals Make You Feel Better,* by John G. Sutton. Copyright © 1998 by John G. Sutton. Published by Element Books, Inc.

"Kirby, My Miracle Worker," by Ed Eames, is used by permission of the author.

"Smokey Bear," "Koko," "The Survivor," "Jumbo," "Morris" and "George L. Mountainlion" are from *Famous Animals of the States,* by Paul D. Buchanan. © 1996 Paul D. Buchanan. Published by McFarland & Company, Inc. Publishers.

"Punxsutawney Phil" and "Scannon, More Than a Mascot" are from *Animals Who Have Won Our Hearts,* by Jean Craighead George. Text copyright © 1994 by Jean Craighead George. Published by HarperCollins Publishers, Inc.

"Cub Life" is from *Born Free,* by Joy Adamson. Copyright © 1960 by Joy Adamson. Published by Pantheon Books, a division of Random House, Inc.

"The Pacing White Mustang" is from *Incredible Animal Adventures* by Jean Craighead George. Text copyright © 1994 by Jean Craighead George. Published by HarperCollins Publishers, Inc.

"Ready to Gallop," by John Fleischman, is from *Smithsonian,* November 1996.

"A Beautiful Stranger" is from *Zarafa,* by Michael Allin. Copyright © 1998 by Michael Allin. Published by Dell Publishing, a division of Random House, Inc.

"Juneau's Official Greeter," by Roberta Sandler, is used by permission of the author.

"Laika, Space Dog" and "Nipper, RCA Dog," by Bonnie Bergen, are from *Animal Fair,* Premiere 1999.

"Pony Express," "Hollywood Hero" and "Ballet on Horseback" are from *Horse Heroes,* by Kate Petty. Copyright © 1999 Dorling Kindersley Limited, London. Published by DK Publishing, Inc.

"Tracker" and "The Champion Nobody Wanted" are from *Shelter Dogs,* by Peg Kehret. Text copyright © 1999 by Peg Kehret. Published by Albert Whitman & Company.

(continued on page 208)

Designed by SMS Typography
Illustrations by Ron Bucalo
Jacket designed by Dennis Arnold
Printed in the United States of America

Contents

A WORLD APART

MOMENTS IN HISTORY

GREAT PERFORMERS

LOVE REMEMBERED

Introduction

Animals become famous for many reasons: their courage and loyalty, their endurance in times of crisis, their special achievements, their intelligence, and sometimes their ability to bring warmth and meaning to our lives. Although we always remember the animals we have known personally, we are also inspired by those who are celebrated. Somehow their examples make us more appreciative of all God's creatures.

In FAMOUS ANIMALS, one of the books in our exclusive series *LISTENING TO THE ANIMALS,* we have gathered many true stories of extraordinary animals. If ever there were a Hall of Fame for Animals, this is it. It is our way of thanking God for the blessings they bring to us.

In *Duty First,* our first chapter, we salute some of the many animals who dedicated their lives to a special purpose. Mary Thurston writes about Sergeant Stubby, a mixed-breed dog who accompanied a regiment of army infantrymen onto the battlefields of World War I and came home a decorated hero. In "Piglet and Richard" we meet a remarkable horse who fights a different kind of battle when he tries to help a disabled young man overcome his self-doubt. And you will be deeply touched by the story of Kirby, a guide dog who lost a leg but not his determination to do his job.

Most of us don't have a chance to get close to the wild animals in *A World Apart,* but we have much to learn from them. It might surprise you to discover that there really was a Smokey Bear, a small cub who survived a terrible forest fire and went on to become a National Forest Service symbol for fire prevention and safe camping practices. You'll also get to know Koko, a gorilla who was trained to use American Sign Language to communicate with people. And, of course, there is Elsa, the lovable lioness raised from a cub by Joy Adamson.

The stories in *Moments in History* introduce us to outstanding animals who were part of our country's past. Paul D. Buchanan writes about a horse named Comanche, the only survivor of the battle of Little Bighorn where General George Custer and his entire party of soldiers died. We also meet Balto and Togo, two dedicated sled dogs who were chosen to pull a sledful of vaccine across the frozen expanse of Alaska to Nome, where an outbreak of diphtheria was threatening the lives of children. The miles were long, the ice and snow treacherous, but no one else could even hope to get through. Another race against time—and danger—was the Pony Express.

In our fourth chapter, *Great Performers,* we rub elbows with celebrities. Raymond Lee's story of Rin Tin Tin explains why the magnificent German Shepherd was one of the first animals to get star billing. We're also introduced to Jumbo, a sweet-natured giant of an elephant who was P. T. Barnum's greatest attraction. And then there is Trigger, Roy Rogers' beloved horse, the most famous animal of his time.

Love Remembered brings us animals who were renowned for their devotion to the people whose lives they shared. Willie Morris lovingly remembers Skip, the dog who was the companion of his boyhood. Enos Mills introduces us to Scotch, the dog who was at his side during many of his most famous wilderness explorations. A mountain lion named George became—yes, it's true!—a columnist for the *Arizona Daily Star.*

As you read about the animals in these fascinating stories, you may begin to realize that they bear a resemblance to the animals you have known and loved. If so, you're quite correct. All of God's creatures bring us closer to him and shower us with his love. Some of them just happen to do it in the spotlight.

PHYLLIS HOBE

FAMOUS ANIMALS

DUTY FIRST

"*Love stretches your heart and makes you big inside.*"

MARGARET ABIGAIL WALKER

$\mathcal{A}$nimals constantly amaze us with their many talents, and they love to put them to use. They particularly like to help us achieve something important. Just ask them to get the paper, guard the house, take a child for a ride, climb a mountain with you or even go to war with you, and they'll do it without hesitation. There's something about responsibility that agrees with them. It's as if they know that's why they're here.

Maybe we can learn something from their ability to put first things first.

A Medal for Tang

TIM JONES

$\mathcal{T}$he friendliness of the giant Newfoundland can be traced through its centuries-old partnership with man. As with many breeds, time has muddied the history of the Newfoundland. They have been traced variously to the Great Pyrenees dogs and to Norwegian sailors who may have brought the dogs to the New World. The most likely history places the Newfoundland in North America long before European contact. Once the dogs roamed wild, from the East Coast to the Great Plains, from Saskatchewan to Mexico. First domesticated by the Algonquins and later by the Sioux, the dogs served as beasts of burden and hunting companions for centuries until the Spanish brought the horse to North America. The name of the breed came from the country where Europeans first encountered them, the island province of Newfoundland off the coast of eastern Canada.

The first European settlers on the island, and the mariners who supplied them, soon discovered the value of these large dogs, who weighed an average of 150 pounds, had long legs with webbed feet, and seemed naturally devoted to human masters. Soon Newfoundlands were hauling carts full of firewood from the forests; helping fishermen drag their heavy nets ashore; and, once it became clear they were talented swimmers and lifesavers, joining the men at sea.

As trade grew along the coast and across the oceans, many ships carried a Newfoundland on board. The dogs were excellent swimmers and natural-born retrievers, so little training was necessary to teach them to dive into the water after equipment or people that had been washed overboard. A drowning sailor would find a Newfoundland suddenly beside him, gripping his clothing in its teeth or maybe just offering its strong back for him to hang onto, as together they struggled back to the ship.

Loyal companions, the dogs were highly valued for their lifesaving abilities. Often they were the first to indicate a landfall, their sensitive noses picking up the scent of shore among the sea breezes. Mostly Newfoundlands traveled with the fishermen exploring the Grand Banks fishing grounds off the coast of Canada, but many traveled the globe even as late as the time of the clipper ships.

The most famous rescue by a Newfoundland came in 1919, when the coastal steamer *Ethie* foundered off the coast of the dogs' namesake island.

Winter storms in the North Atlantic generate not only raging winds and mountainous seas but also driving, blinding snow to complicate the mariner's voyage. Along the rocky coast of the Canadian Maritimes, spires reach up through the water to rip out the bottom of any unfortunate vessels caught near the shore.

In December of 1919, the *Ethie* fought a snowstorm within a gale until she came into the surf close to Martin's Point in Bonne Bay on the coast of Newfoundland. With over ninety people aboard, the steamship went aground on the rocks off shore and lay at the mercy of the pounding waves. Rockets fired by the crew alerted people ashore, who came to the beach to help with the rescue. What they needed was a connection, some way to move the passengers and crew safely from the ship to the shore.

The crew attempted to shoot one of the ship's lines to the people on the beach, but it fell short. Then a sailor took a rope and jumped into the surf, attempting to swim the lifeline to the beach. Waves swept him away, and he was never seen again. The passengers and crew aboard the *Ethie* stood so near to shore, yet so far.

That's when the ship's Newfoundland, Tang, caught the attention of the captain. One has to wonder what the captain thought. Perhaps he'd heard stories about Newfoundlands but never actually had seen one perform. He was running out of choices. The captain ordered the crew to retrieve the lifeline and give the end to Tang. Taking the line in his teeth, the dog plunged into the surf and headed toward shore.

In those gale-driven waters, Tang must have struggled, the waves pounding against him, the undertow trying to drag him out to sea. He swam on, shaking the salt water out of his eyes, until he approached the beach. Some of the rescue party waded into the surf and reached the dog. They took the line from his mouth and fastened it to a strong point. With the connection made, the ship's crew quickly rigged up a system of ropes and pulleys and attached to it a "breeches buoy," a seat made out of a pair of short pants hanging inside a round life preserver. One by one, sitting inside the breeches buoy, ninety-one people aboard the *Ethie* were shuttled over the waves to the shore.

An infant presented a problem. If the baby's mother carried him in her arms, then was dipped into the surf, the child might be torn away by the strength of the waves. Instead, creative sailors fixed a mailbag to the lifeline and put the baby inside. Safe in his bag, the baby was pulled along the lifeline to the waiting hands of his rescuers.

History doesn't record what Tang did once he'd made his way to shore, but it's not hard to picture the excited dog searching for his master, greeting every passenger that descended from the breeches buoy. Lloyd's of London, the famous insurance agency, later awarded the brave dog with a medal for Meritorious Service, which he wore on his collar for the rest of his life.

The *New York Times* reported the rescue a week later, citing communications difficulties because the storm had knocked down all power and communications lines. In the article, Tang was credited with saving ninety-two lives, perhaps the largest number of lives saved by any dog in a single incident.

from DOG HEROES

Beyond Appearances

ERIC SWANSON

"*A*n animal's eyes have the power to speak a great language," the twentieth-century philosopher Martin Buber once observed. Few humans have enjoyed the privilege of witnessing the profound effect of this unique form of communication as closely as Sandra Campbell. A registered nurse, Campbell is a longtime volunteer with the animal-assisted therapy program sponsored by the Somerset, New Jersey, Humane Society (a.k.a. St. Hubert's Giralda). Since the inception of the program in 1990, she's taken kittens from the shelter to convalescent centers, nursing homes, VA units, and senior residences in the Somerset County area, visiting patients typically considered to have passed beyond the reach of conventional medical assistance. The men and women she sees often suffer from advanced forms of Alzheimer's disease, psychiatric disorders, or irreversible physical traumas.

For several years, one of her most talented assistants has been a gray tabby named Spunky. Like the rest of the kittens who accompanied Sandra to various facilities, Spunky was returned to the shelter at the end of every visit. Unlike the others, however, the little gray fellow with ears too big for his head just couldn't seem to get himself adopted. Day after day, he watched his more attractive and outgoing compatriots carried off in the arms of excited human companions; day after day, he was left behind, like the kid chosen last for the school baseball team.

Finally, Sandra couldn't stand the sorry spectacle any longer, and she and her husband, Barry, decided to adopt Spunky themselves. She trained the kitten to lie on a towel, which became a kind of portable "safe" zone to be taken along on visiting days. Spread out on a floor, a table, a hospital bed, or the lap of an elderly patient, the towel symbolized an appropriate place to be; Spunky sat wherever it was laid, happily accepting the attention lavished on him by grateful patients.

Staff and administrators at the facilities Spunky visited were amazed both by his serenity and by the effect he had on patients. Many of the patients he came in contact with suffered from varying degrees of agitation. Those who could still recognize their surroundings worried about their health, while those whose memories had failed suffered from the terrible anxiety and confusion that results from memory loss. With Spunky gazing up at them from their laps, patients gradually relaxed, forgot their troubles, and became focused on the present moment. Some began telling stories about cherished animal companions of their own; others felt themselves transported back to pleasant scenes of distant times.

A year or so after adopting Spunky, Sandra was working in the shelter when someone dropped off an abandoned kitten. Thunderstorms had raged all afternoon, and the tiny orange fur ball was a wet and woeful sight, positively crawling with fleas, yet purring loudly enough to be heard across the entire reception room. Later that night, Sandra happened to mention the uncomely little creature to her husband, Barry. Something in her description tugged at Barry, and he suggested that they go back to the shelter the next day "just to take a look." Anyone with even a moderate understanding of human psychology will have foreseen by this point that the Campbells did not return home empty-handed.

The little orange fur ball, impressively christened Ralph Syracuse Campbell, soon began to serve as Spunky's understudy, visiting patients when the older cat was feeling low. For several years now the pair has worked as a team, accompanying Sandra on alternate days to various residences and health care facilities. Whereas Spunky tends to stretch comfortably out on a patient's lap, Ralph likes to play "the invisible game," tucking his face inside an elbow or a hand until he's sure his winsome, shy demeanor has completely won over whoever's holding him.

Yet despite the difference in their individual styles, both cats seem particularly proficient at drawing out patients who suffer from extreme forms of Alzheimer's or dementia. In one exemplary case, Spunky jumped onto the lap of an elderly woman who had lapsed into a completely nonverbal state. Startling the nurses who had grown accustomed to her silence, the old woman smiled down at her visitor and remarked, "Pretty cat." The following week, when Ralph stepped gingerly onto her lap, the old woman uttered her first complete sentence in years. Meeting Ralph's coyly upturned gaze, she exclaimed, "My, what a handsome cat this is!"

The mystery of silent communication between man and animal may never be fully understood. It can, however, be rewarded. In 1995, the Delta Society honored Ralph and Spunky with an award for Lifetime Achievement in the field of animal-assisted therapy. Their uncanny gift for breaking through bar-

riers others have found impenetrable is a lesson to us all—and
a sign of hope that beyond the confusing babble of grunts and
cries that daily arises among the creatures of the earth, a single
great language may truly unite us all.

from HERO CATS

Sergeant Stubby

MARY THURSTON

During World War I, in the summer of 1917, a homeless dog wandered into the training camp of the army's 102nd Infantry at Yale University. The young boxer mix quickly endeared himself to the troops, particularly Private J. Robert Conroy, and was adopted as an unofficial member of the division. They named him Stubby, after his stub of a tail. Despite a "no pets allowed" policy, Stubby shared meals and sleeping quarters with the men and reportedly began mimicking their drills and marching exercises.

When it came time to go to war, Conroy and his colleagues smuggled the dog aboard a steamer headed for Europe. Stubby reached the trenches of the front line in February, 1916, in the midst of a horrific battle. Although he had no formal training to cope with such nightmarish conditions, he calmly endured an unceasing barrage of shelling for the first 30 days. Stubby's caretakers were amazed by his cool under fire and were absolutely stunned when he voluntarily ventured out into the battle zone to seek out and comfort wounded soldiers still caught in the crossfire. News of the dog's bravery and heroism reached the French village of Domrémy, and after fighting subsided, the women of the town presented him with a hand-sewn chamois coat decorated with Allied flags and his name stitched in gold thread.

By war's end, Stubby had been credited numerous times with saving his regiment from certain disaster. He would warn the men of incoming mortar shells by barking or hurling himself to the ground. One time, he prevented the escape of a German spy by sinking his teeth into the seat of the man's pants, refusing to let go. Whiffs of mustard gas, too faint to be detected by the human nose, sent Stubby into a barking tirade that warned soldiers to don protective gear. Stubby roused a sleeping soldier just in time to get both his and the soldier's mask on. The regiment had provided Stubby with his own makeshift gas mask, custom-fitted to accommodate his round head and flattened snout.

Stubby was also an experienced "therapy dog" long before animal visitations were proven to hasten the recovery time of the sick or seriously injured. He ministered to the troops in his own canine fashion, often cuddling up to wounded or shell-shocked soldiers, keeping them warm through a long winter's night. Sometimes, he simply sat staring intently into the men's faces, his piercing hypnotic gaze calming and distracting them from their pain or grief. During a lull in the fighting at Toul, France, Stubby took it upon himself to get out of his little bed and wander through the field hospital, visiting soldiers who, like him, were recovering from injuries received in the line of fire.

At one point, Conroy was wounded and evacuated to a hospital in Paris. Hospital administrators granted an exception to their "no pets" rule and allowed Stubby to keep his friend company. Medics found Stubby's conduct impeccable, and the cathartic effect of his visits was noted by the physicians. On extended convalescence leave with Conroy in France, Stubby's fame continued to grow. He became the toast of Paris when he saved a little girl from being run over in the middle of a busy thoroughfare and was frequently seen strolling about town wearing his chamois blanket, which now sported a rapidly growing array of honorary medals donated by friends and admirers.

Eighteen months after Stubby debarked on foreign soil, the war came to an end. He had served in at least 18 major battles and saw more action than most human soldiers. Back home, Stubby became a nationally acclaimed hero and eventually was received by Presidents Wilson, Harding, and Coolidge. General Pershing presented him with a gold medal and declared him a "hero of the highest caliber."

Despite his nationwide fame, Stubby at times encountered prejudice against his kind—a mutt. In 1923, thousands of spectators hoping to see the little hero packed a national dog show in Boston. Breeders attempted to block his guest appearance, complaining that he was a mongrel and therefore had no business at an exhibition of pedigreed dogs. A show judge ruled against them, saying, "He may be a mutt, but he's done more than all of your dogs put together—Stubby stays!"

from PETS: PART OF THE FAMILY

Boo's Challenge

KENT AND DONNA DANNEN

$\mathcal{K}$aribou, nicknamed Boo, was the first dog to win the Samoyed Club of America's highest working award. He had led many Samoyed sled teams, had earned SCA's annual award for Top Samoyed Sled Dog, and had won the Sled Dog Class at various Samoyed specialty dog shows. He had also carried packs equaling 25 percent of his weight to many high passes and summits in Colorado's Indian Peaks Wilderness. But he had never hiked the 11,851-foot tundra meadows and cliff-hugging trail of Caribou Pass.

A dozen years earlier, the grandeur of Caribou Pass had impressed us so much that we had named our prized puppy for the place. Details, responsibilities, and coincidences of life had kept us from climbing back to the pass with its namesake who made countless other wilderness excursions much easier and much more rewarding.

Boo had turned twelve in early fall and was slowing down. Injury and kidney disease had conspired with time to make him an old dog, but they had not made him content to relax in non-working retirement. His chief delight still was to enrich his owners' wilderness experiences. Our hopes turned again to the pass we had not visited for many years. Could we lead Boo to his namesake place? Was he still fit enough to make the climb?

Neither we, nor Boo, nor two younger Samoyed pack dogs Glacier Lily and Maroon Belle, could hike far beyond the wilderness boundary when an early snowstorm frustrated our first attempt. As we loaded the dogs into our minivan, a coyote trotted across the trailhead parking lot, barely visible in the blowing snow and fog. All three dogs and the coyote seemed to share satisfaction and contentment with retreating before the storm. They were all at peace in recognizing when to quit, more at peace than we humans were, and we learned from their acceptance.

John Muir, we remembered, had shared a stormy experience with the dog Stickeen in the Alaskan wilderness of Glacier Bay National Park and gained significant insights from his canine companion. Muir wrote of the dog, "through him as through a window I have ever since been looking with deeper sympathy into all my fellow mortals." This sympathy made Muir the most famous advocate for conservation of wilderness, wilderness that converted dogs into windows to the otherwise invisible viewpoint of wild animals.

When we started up the path to Caribou Pass a few days later, the wild animals were active as they emerged from suppression by the autumn snow. Boo often alerted us to things he had smelled or heard along the trail. We noted a yellow-rumped warbler, now dressed in its drab fall feathers, about to head south. Farther up the trail, a pika scurried among the rocks, eager to complete the harvest of flowers that would be winter food.

Mostly, though, we guessed about the canine translation of what Aldo Leopold, a founder of the Wilderness Society and of the profession of wildlife management, called "olfactory poems that who-knows-what silent creatures have written in the . . . night." He once wrote, "My dog . . . persists in tutoring me with the calm patience of a professor of logic, in the art of drawing deductions from an educated nose. I delight in seeing him deduce a conclusion, in the form of a point, from data that are obvious to him, but speculative to my unaided eye. Perhaps he hopes his dull pupil will one day learn to smell."

Most modern adherents to Leopold's land ethic who wonder at the wisdom revealed in his classic *Sand County Almanac,* do not take seriously his self-description as a "dull pupil." Years after the climb to Caribou Pass, however, we heard from Nina Leopold Bradley that her father meant what he wrote. He could gain so much wisdom from the wilds, she said, because his modesty let him learn from his dogs.

If Leopold's German shorthaired pointer was a professor of logic, Karibou was a professor of geography. Bred by Arctic nomads to pull sleds, carry packs, and herd reindeer over long distances, Karibou's breed was not inclined to stationary pointing. Our Samoyeds preferred to pull their owners up the trail and over the ridge.

Secured by leashes to our waists, the dogs practically lifted us up the steep trail, making our journey seem easier and shorter than when we had hiked it without a sled dog boost. Our packs were lighter as well, for the dogs hauled some of the necessary gear in their packs, leaving room in ours for guidebooks, binoculars, and cameras to better understand and enjoy the riches offered by Indian Peaks.

It was an advantage obvious to hikers we encountered at the abandoned Fourth of July Mine. They laughingly asked to buy our dogs on the spot but had to be content with just photographing them.

The rusted bits of mining machinery near tree line turned

our thoughts to those who had preceded us in the wilds by as much as 11,000 years, people whose motives and attitudes towards the wilderness were necessarily different from ours. We were the first wilderness travelers who did not view these mountains as human habitat from which a living had to be wrenched. Earning a living here was hard; and death for a variety of reasons was not surprising. Those of us who saw Indian Peaks as a recreational resource, however, got our food from supermarkets and expected protection from high-tech gear and rangers.

If the ghost of a Paleolithic mammoth hunter had hidden in the dwarf willows and watched two groups of modern hikers at Fourth of July Mine, our technology and motives would have been as strange as though we had descended from the stars. The hiding ghost, however, would have joined in admiration of Karibou, Glacier, and Rooney, and would have recognized the leashes and dog packs as his own tools.

The dogs were tremendously important for us because they were our only link to the past, a link that was necessary to give us a sense of belonging in the wilds. Without this reference point, many other wilderness values would have faded.

Our friends of the moment passed from the mine down the trail, and we resumed hiking toward Caribou Pass, pulled upward by our dogs. High on the tundra near the rock-rimmed tarn, Lake Dorothy, we met a young woman hiking alone with her yellow Labrador retriever. The dog wore no pack, and his red leash was not attached to his owner's waist. She also was traveling pretty light, with a small pack and the long-legged, lithe build of a runner.

Perhaps her dog supplied the sense of security desired by many women and some men who prefer to hike alone. Because people who hike alone presumably prefer to be alone, we did no more than greet the young woman and her lab in passing. We did not really know if her dog was along for security or just for fun.

In the company of dogs, a hiker can have the benefits of solitude from other people without the natural discomfort of solitude. Dogs are pack animals and can provide us humans with the pack's sense of well-being and security without compromising the benefits of wilderness solitude.

Moreover, dogs can enhance the sense of solitude that sometimes is hard to come by in any wilderness area with unavoidably high visitation. Most of these visitors come from an urban environment where they have learned, with justification, to be wary of strangers. Such wariness usually is of slight value in the wilds, but good urban habits are hard to leave behind at the trailhead. More by their companionship than by their real defensive value, dogs can help hikers reduce their fear of other wilderness visitors who are present but probably not dangerous.

Sometimes, however, the danger may be real. Donna and a female friend were hiking in the Never Summer Range on the west edge of Rocky Mountain National Park. Denied canine companions by national park rules, they had to leave Karibou home.

They missed him greatly when some presumably drunken men saw them from cliffs above and decided it was clever or alluring to yell obscenities and roll down boulders on the women. Donna and her friend evaded the rocks easily as they retreated down the valley. What they could not evade was extreme mental discomfort as they camped that night. Karibou, who looked like a small, white wolf despite his friendly disposition, would have restored much of the peace that men had stolen from those women.

But on this trip Karibou was with us, and he answered easily our question about his fitness to climb to Caribou Pass. We, however, did not lead him there. He led us and answered in many ways many other questions that we had not known to ask. Just for the fun of it, he led us a half mile farther for a different view of Caribou Lake far below and across its deep valley to glacier-carved, snow-dusted Apache and Navajo peaks. Karibou led us to his namesake pass, making the trip easy, fun, informative, and inspirational. We should not have been surprised; he had performed these services for us throughout his long canine life. He would do so again.

Piglet and Richard

JOHN G. SUTTON

Throughout the world there are places where people with disabilities can go to enjoy the therapeutic experience of being with animals. Within Dartmoor National Park in the county of Devon, England, high on a hill overlooking the mysterious moorland is just such a place. At the end of a steep, winding lane, where the woodlands part into a cobbled farmyard, is the Camomile Centre, founded by Helen Cottington. It is the most wonderful place. There are horses to ride, donkeys, a lovely pony, hens, rabbits, dogs, and even a little vegetable garden.

One of the resident therapy horses at the Camomile Centre is called Piglet. He is quite a big horse, very strong and fifteen hands in height. This chestnut cob has a beautiful flaxen mane and tail which he swishes from side to side whenever he greets his special friends. One of Piglet's friends is an eighteen-year-old called Richard Holman. Richard lives in a little town near Bovey Tracey, just a few miles from the center. He visits the center at least once a week to ride.

I saw them together on a rainy day early in August 1997. Dartmoor was shrouded in the kind of mist that makes one think of the Hound of the Baskervilles and haunted castles. At three o'clock Richard arrived, holding his hard hat. He was looking forward to riding his favorite horse, Piglet. Richard's father Peter watched with a degree of pride as his son tried to place his riding hat on his head. The center staff supervised Richard and prepared him for his equestrian adventure. Outside in the yard Piglet was patiently waiting.

Then Piglet trotted ahead to the paddock from the yard and Richard followed, with the staff close at hand. Watching the young man making his way to ride Piglet, I was aware that this was what he wanted to do. I could sense the determination in each of his faltering, often hesitant steps. He walked with great difficulty, being severely physically disabled, but he walked. There was fun at the end of this little journey and Richard was going to get there.

Inside the wood-fenced arena, assisted by the staff, Richard climbed up on the mounting platform and was helped into the horse's saddle. Being totally deaf and almost completely blind, he lives under close supervision. Whenever his parents are not by his side, there are trained staff and carers to watch over him. Except when he is riding Piglet. On top of that horse Richard is alone, as independent as he will ever be.

As soon as Piglet felt Richard's hand on him, the horse turned and swished his flaxen mane, brushing it softly against his fingers. The horse's tail swung up and flicked from side to side as if welcoming his friend. All these little signals seemed to register on Richard's face as his senses tuned in to the happy experience of being on horseback. With his hands gripping the saddle and his feet firmly in the stirrups, Richard was ready to ride.

As if someone in the heavens had been watching for this moment, the rain stopped. The clouds parted and sunshine shone down on the woods and green, rolling hills. In the far distance, as the sun lifted the drifting mist, we could see the

Dartmoor marsh grass leading out to Cornwall and the far-away sea.

The staff took Piglet's reins and led him out of the paddock into the lane. At each turn of the path the horse halted and checked his rider. At one junction he stopped dead still, his ears pricking up. No one moved. Then a car turned the corner into the path where we would have been but for Piglet. He had obviously heard the oncoming vehicle and had acted to protect his friend in the saddle.

I could see the concentration on Richard's face. He was balanced perfectly on that horse. For mile after mile he rode, up hill and down the thorn-hedged paths across the moors, circling the Camomile Centre. Piglet appeared to understand exactly what was required of him with regard to giving his friend Richard a safe ride. The special care was evident in each step the horse took.

In the paddock Richard's father was waiting, together with Helen Cottington. When Richard returned, they watched as the staff helped him off Piglet. Then he walked slowly back and gripped the safety of his father's arm. On Richard's face there was just the hint of a secret smile. He had enjoyed the ride. "You did well, son," said Peter. Although Richard could not hear, I knew that he understood. I think Piglet did too, for as we walked together into the farmyard stables, the big horse shook its glorious mane and whinnied in that funny way horses only do when they are absolutely happy.

from *ANIMALS MAKE YOU FEEL BETTER*

The Bravest Cat in the World

ERIC SWANSON

Though cats certainly have played their part in a number of great naval battles, few have been tested quite as severely on the home front as a gallant little tabby named Faith. Her youth remains a mystery. Faith was a stray who wandered into the London church of St. Augustine and St. Faith on Watling Street one cold, wet afternoon in 1936. Perhaps she'd been abandoned by her original owners, who, like so many well-intentioned persons during the Depression era, simply lacked the means to care for themselves, much less their cherished dependents.

The church caretaker attempted several times to remove the little tabby from the premises. Her insistence on hearing Mass, however, and her sweet, somewhat shy manner captivated St. Augustine's rector, Reverend Henry Ross. Ross insisted that the cat be allowed to remain, and he even made a bed and litter box available in his room on the third floor of the rectory. Reverend Ross himself chose the name that would make Faith famous as an international symbol of wartime fortitude.

From the day she arrived at St. Augustine, Faith became a model parishioner, attending Mass regularly and welcoming newcomers and longtime church members alike. At the beginning of each service, she took part in the procession down the aisle, and afterward chose a seat at the very front of the church. When Reverend Ross delivered his sermon, Faith would rise from her pew and curl at his feet—perhaps not so much to keep an eye on the congregation as to inspire wakefulness in those inclined to sleep.

Toward the end of the summer of 1940, her attendance became somewhat irregular—not through any lapse of devotion, but rather as a result of her delicate condition. As August drew to a close, Faith gave birth to a single black and white kitten. Inspired by the new arrival's coloring, the rector and his staff decided to name the little male Panda, after the favorite attraction then on display at the London Zoological Society.

As Hitler's troops marched across Europe, a sense of nervous anticipation settled over England. Food, coal, and other precious commodities had been rationed since the beginning of the year. In May 1940, Holland and Belgium surrendered to the German troops, followed by France in June. In July, the Germans began bombing the British coast, steadily working their way inland to destroy railroads and factories.

Since the feline predictive capabilities have yet to be thoroughly explored, no one can say with any certainty what inspired Faith to bring her kitten to a safer spot inside the rectory. Three days before the great bombing of London, she insisted on carrying Panda by the scruff of the neck from the third floor to a sort of recess or pigeonhole in the basement. Following her down to the basement, Reverend Ross watched them settle into the recess, which was protected in part by stacks of old organ music. Fearing, however, that Faith and her newborn might catch cold in the cellar, the rector carried mother and kitten back to their warm bed beside the fireplace in his room.

Faith returned to the cellar three more times before Reverend Ross finally gave in and had her bed and litter box brought down to the basement recess.

Three nights later, on September 8, 1940, the Germans dropped their bombs on the city of London. St. Augustine stood directly in the shadow of St. Paul's cathedral, the principal target of the German bombs. The entire area around the great cathedral erupted in a hellish scene of carnage, twisted metal, and incinerating flames. Reverend Ross was in Westminster at the time of the bombing. The next morning, he hurried back to London to find that St. Augustine had taken a direct hit. A German bomb had pierced the roof of the rectory, and most of the building had collapsed in flames.

Firemen on the scene forbade Reverend Ross from searching the burning debris for Faith and Panda, telling him in no uncertain terms that the cat and her kitten couldn't have survived the bomb. Reverend Ross stood staring hopelessly at the smoking ruins until the firemen were called away to another emergency. The rector then picked his way through the burning remains, calling for Faith.

The basement recess where Faith had chosen to spend the previous three nights was completely covered by rubble. As he neared the spot, however, Reverend Ross heard Faith answering his cry. He seized an axe that had been left behind by the firemen and chopped through the smoldering timbers and shingles. Faith lay quite still in her cubbyhole, using her own body to shield Panda from the smoke and flames. She watched calmly as Reverend Ross made his way toward the pair.

"Her attitude," he described later, "said unmistakably, 'Why haven't you come to fetch us sooner?'"

With the aid of a fireman, he pulled mother and kitten

completely unharmed from the wreckage, only moments before the remaining wall of the rectory collapsed, completely
engulfing the recess in flames and smoke. Ross carried his
charges into the vestry tower, which was still standing. There,
Faith began licking herself and Panda. According to the rector,
she paused every once in a while to lift her head and sing
"such a song of praise and thanksgiving as I had never heard
from her before."

When Panda grew old enough to be separated from his
mother, he was given to a nursing home in Herne Hill, where
his company cheered patients recovering from devastating ill-
nesses. Meanwhile, as the war dragged on, Faith's example of
simple courage and devotion during the bombing became an
inspiration to her neighbors and other visitors to the church. In
time, Reverend Ross hung her picture in the tower chapel,
where services were held until the church was rebuilt. Underneath, he posted an inscription that read in part:

> *Our dear little church cat of St. Augustine and St. Faith,*
> *the bravest cat in the world. On Monday, September*
> *9, 1940, she endured horrors and perils beyond the*
> *power of words to tell. Shielding her kitten in a sort of*
> *recess in the house . . . she sat the whole frightful night*
> *of bombing and fire, guarding her little kitten. The*
> *roofs and masonry exploded, the whole house blazed,*
> *four floors fell through in front of her. Fire and water*
> *and ruin all around her. Yet she stayed calm and*
> *steadfast and waited for help . . .*

Gradually, Faith's story began to circulate more widely,
appearing in various newspapers and journals. On the fifth

anniversary of the terrible night, her picture and a brief recapitulation of the events appeared in the London *Evening News*. Ultimately, the story came to the attention of Maria Dickin, who, together with Dorothea St. Hill Bourne of the Allied Forces' Mascot Club, decided to bestow a special honor on the little tabby.

Because Faith wasn't an official member of the armed services or civil defense, she was ineligible for the Dickin Medal. However, Mrs. Dickin created a special silver medal engraved with the words:

> *From the PDSA to Faith of St. Augustine's Watling Street, E.C. For steadfast courage in the Battle of London, September 9, 1940.*

A certificate was also drawn up, recognizing Faith's courage under fire. Faith received both the certificate and the medal on October 12, 1945, during a special service at St. Augustine, attended by Mrs. Dickin and the Archbishop of Canterbury.

The following year, the Greenwich Village Humane League of New York sent another citation for courage, along with the Paddy Reilly Silver Medal of Honor. By all accounts, Faith remained a humble, steadfast parishioner of the newly rebuilt St. Augustine church. Yet even her quiet end on September 28, 1948, made headlines, as newspapers and journals around the world reported the sad news that "The Bravest Cat in the World" had passed away.

from HERO CATS

The Earthquake Dog

JOHN G. SUTTON

In 1968 Linda Watt moved with her family to the town of Newhall in California. Her sons Shannon and Gregory were then ten and eleven. The boys wanted a pet, so Linda took them to the local animal shelter. They picked out a beautiful long-haired German shepherd, and called her Gertrude.

The boys just loved Gertrude. Other dogs loved her too— lots of them. Soon Gertrude gave birth to puppies. There were twelve in all, six dogs and six bitches. They had the most wonderful coats: six were almost pure white and the others black and tan. The boys were sad when Linda explained that the family couldn't possibly keep them all, and the puppies were sold.

Before long, Gertrude was pregnant again. Linda had tried to keep her in, but Gertrude could jump right over the garden's seven-foot fence. In due course she gave birth to twelve more cute pups. Again Linda sold them to the townsfolk of Newhall. But this constant breeding had to stop! The town was filling up with cross-breed dogs.

The next time Gertrude came into season, Linda persuaded the local vet to lock her up in his secure kennels at the rear of his practice. That would keep Gertrude out of trouble, Linda thought.

She was wrong. The very first night Gertrude was locked in the kennels, she broke out. Not only that, but somehow she opened all the other dogs' cages and they ran free. Then Gertrude celebrated her escape by mating with General, the vet's huge pedigree German shepherd show dog. The vet was not amused.

This time Gertrude gave birth to thirteen pups. The last one to be born was the runt of the litter. It was all wrinkly and weak, and hadn't got a hair on its body. The vet said it was certain to die, and Gertrude would not nurse it. But Linda wanted it to live. She used a glass eye-drop dispenser to feed the tiny creature milk and honey, water, and even some whiskey. The puppy was so small it could barely swallow, but it struggled and fought for its life. So hard did it try that the boys called it Captain Courageous, or Cappy for short.

Once again Linda sold all the healthy pups off, but Cappy, who was still very weak, became her own favorite little pet. Each day she would feed him and stroke his newly grown white coat. Cappy would push his tiny wet nose into Linda's hand and lick her fingers, just as he had done as a day-old pup. . . .

On February 2nd, 1972, at 4:49 A.M. Western U.S. time, Linda woke from a deep sleep to find Cappy on the bed, standing on her stomach. The dog was growling and crying in a pitiful way, pulling and tugging at Linda's nightgown as if trying to drag her out of bed.

Linda was shocked. What, she wondered, could Cappy want at this time in the morning? He always slept downstairs and hated beds, so there was obviously something wrong. Then the dog jumped off the bed and ran out through the door, heading toward her sons' room.

It was then that she heard a booming crack which she recognized as being the start of an earthquake. As fast as she could, Linda dashed into the boys' bedroom and got them out of bed. Quickly they ran downstairs out of the house and into the middle of the garden.

There were more loud underground explosions. Suddenly, amid flashes and sparks, everywhere was plunged into total darkness as the electricity lines came crashing down. From where the Watt family stood on the lawn, they could see, in the moonlight, the house shaking like a tree in a high wind. The ground was heaving and trembling beneath their feet.

Cappy was there with them, making sure they were all right. He was barking with excitement, jumping up and licking the boys' faces. They were safe, and he had helped save them.

For five days Linda, her sons, and all the townsfolk were trapped within the valley because the roads leading in and out had collapsed. Many homes were damaged beyond repair. The earthquake had measured 6.9 on the Richter scale and their town was just four miles from the epicentre.

During the days they were trapped, the area suffered numerous aftershocks. Cappy seemed able to predict these just as he had the main one. From sitting quite still, he would quickly stand up, turning round and round on the spot, looking hard at the ground. Each time he did this, within ten minutes, a minor earthquake followed. Because so many houses were in ruins, other families temporarily shared the Watts' home. They all saw Cappy behaving this way. He became known as Cappy, the earthquake dog, and everyone in the area knew of his ability to predict quakes.

One night, about three days after the initial shock, Cappy started his by now familiar routine of jumping up and running round on the spot. Everyone watched the dog and looked at the clock. Seven minutes passed, no quake; eight minutes passed, nothing; nine minutes, total silence—the tension was terrible. Just as the second hand swept to mark ten minutes, one woman who could stand it no longer shouted "SHAKE, SHAKE!" at the top of her voice. She nearly collapsed as the earth began to tremble underneath her. Cappy had been right again.

Cappy repeated his earthquake-warning dance many, many times throughout his life and he was never wrong once. If ever there was an impending earth tremor over 3 points on the Richter scale, Cappy would dance.

Linda Watt is quite certain that the German shepherd saved her and her sons' lives that dreadful night in 1972. When she examined the house after the quake, all the wardrobes in the bedrooms had fallen over and smashed into the beds. If her boys had been in there asleep, they and she might easily have been killed. Little Captain Courageous had more than repaid Linda and her sons for saving his life all those years before, when he had been the last puppy, the runt of the litter.

from ANIMALS MAKE YOU FEEL BETTER

Kirby, My Miracle Worker

ED EAMES

$\mathcal{K}$irby was nearly three years old when we met. I needed a new guide dog and he needed a partner. He had been trained by Guide Dogs of the Desert, in Palm Springs, and was working with an older blind man. Then the man fell and had to go home without Kirby, but he made the training director promise to keep the marvelous Golden Retriever for him. Just a few weeks before I applied for a new guide dog, Kirby's potential partner decided not to continue with his training. Had I not applied at just that time, Kirby would have been released from the program and placed as a pet in a loving home.

There is a Yiddish word, *beshert,* which means "fated to be," and that's the way I felt about Kirby from the moment we met. He had waited for me, and I was still deep in mourning at the loss of my previous guide dog, a black Labrador Retriever named Perrier. As Kirby and I took up our lives together under the watchful eyes of the training staff, my admiration and love for this marvelous 78-pound bundle of joy and affection grew day by day.

The culminating event in our bonding process took place one day on the streets of Banning, a nearby town where students regularly trained with their new canine partners. As Kirby guided me across the street, a woman driver, blinded by the afternoon sun, made a left turn directly into our path. My new partner stopped on a dime, and I could feel the rear fender of the car as it brushed my leg. Trainer Kathy Laber said she never saw a closer call in her 20 years of guide dog work.

After graduation, we returned to my home in Fresno, California, where Kirby became part of the family. His siblings were Ivy, my wife Toni's Golden Retriever guide dog, and our cats Kimmel and Disney. Toni and I had a very busy schedule writing and lecturing about animals trained to assist the disabled, and as our careers blossomed, we and our partners traveled the country.

Three years later, when Kirby was six, I noticed that he had a slight limp in his left foreleg. I took him to Dr. Helen Hamilton, an internist at a specialty veterinary hospital in Santa Cruz, California, but when she examined him she found no visible cause for a limp and suggested it might be a pulled muscle.

Early the next month I flew to Washington, D.C., to participate in the National Federation of the Blind's "Educate Congress Week." Kirby handled the trip with his usual aplomb until a full day of walking the halls of Congress left him sadly limping and in obvious pain. For the first time the source of his discomfort could be located: I felt a bulging of the bone in the lower part of his left front leg.

Realizing Kirby was in pain and couldn't guide effectively, I flew home a day early and took him to our local veterinarian, Dr. Bob Larsen. X rays showed that an aggressive tumor had destroyed most of the ulna bone. Hearing the dreaded word *cancer* threw Toni and me into the depths of despair. When we asked Dr. Larsen about treatment, and heard the word *amputation,* I felt as if my world was crumbling.

We took Kirby back to the specialty hospital for a biopsy to determine the type of cancer and the course of treatment. Then we waited for the results. We also consulted Dr. Steve Withro, a Colorado-based expert on limb salvage, and Dr. Ann Jeglum, a Pennsylvania-based research oncologist. We were still reaching for that impossible dream, treatment without amputation. But it was not to be. On February 12, 1993, our friend Michelle Price drove us and Kirby to Santa Cruz for chemotherapy and the subsequent amputation of his left front leg and shoulder.

All the way to the hospital, Toni and I struggled with the idea that we were subjecting our beautiful, happy-go-lucky Golden Retriever partner in independence to such a radical mutilation of his body. However, deep down we knew we had no other option.

It was extremely sad dealing with Kirby when he returned home. Although I heard many stories about the feats of three-legged dogs, they were hard to believe. He was reluctant to move unless coaxed to do so. The only exception was at feeding time. The day we brought Kirby home from the veterinary hospital, he was so lethargic, we didn't think he would be interested in eating. What an underestimation of his Golden Retrieverness!

We always required Kirby and Ivy to maintain a down-stay under the dining-room table while their food was being prepared. Ivy's bowl was placed on the floor to the right of the kitchen counter and Kirby's on the left. They would wait, drooling and quivering, for the signal to eat.

At the first home feeding after the surgery, Ivy waited under the table, as usual, but we left Kirby stretched out in the middle of the living-room floor. To our amazement, at the *eat* signal, Kirby jumped over Ivy to get to his bowl! We then realized nothing would keep Kirby down for long!

Day by day, we saw marked improvement in Kirby's ability to ambulate. He no longer had to be encouraged to join us upstairs in the computer room or to go outdoors for relief.

A month after the amputation, Kirby had regained a great deal of strength and stamina, but still did not roll or play one of his favorite games: chasing Kimmel, our cat. Meanwhile, Kimmel used all of his feline wiles to induce Kirby to chase him. It was painful for us to see Kirby remaining motionless while Kimmel rubbed back and forth across Kirby's face and chest. About two weeks later, we startled a guest when we let out whoops of joy at the sound of Kirby chasing Kimmel throughout the house!

I hated leaving Kirby home during this recuperative period. When Toni harnessed Ivy, Kirby came hopping to the front door expecting to accompany us. Never imagining he could actually guide, I took him with us one day to our favorite Chinese restaurant, Wang's Panda, where the proprietor, Jeffrey Wang, has always been delighted to see our dogs. After getting out of our friend's car, I reflexively picked up the harness handle and, to my amazement, Kirby guided me to the restaurant door!

This surprising experience left me confused about Kirby's future. I began to question our assumption that he would have to be retired as my guide. Back in February, when Kirby was diagnosed with bone cancer, I thought his career as a guide was over. I had made arrangements to train with a successor dog at Kansas Specialty Dog Service in Washington, Kansas. Now, I began to dream that our next trip to KSDS would be for a friendly visit and to demonstrate Kirby's new-found skills as a three-legged guide dog!

At a lecture we presented to the veterinary students at the University of California, Davis, we received a great deal of encouragement to rehabilitate Kirby as a guide. Bolstered by the veterinary students' positive outlook, we began exploring the possibility of starting a rehabilitation program, despite the necessity for three post-surgical chemotherapy treatments.

Before making any firm decision, we consulted several surgical veterinary specialists who advised us to build Kirby's stamina and muscles by taking him for long walks and giving him the opportunity to run. Since these activities would place additional stress on his hips, we had them x rayed. With no signs of dysplasia, we explored ways to initiate an exercise program.

I did not want to take long walks with Kirby in harness because I believed this would put undue pressure on him. An acquaintance suggested her nineteen-year-old brother, Kent Phelps, might be interested in assuming the responsibility for walking Kirby. Kent's Labrador had been in a fatal accident in Oklahoma and, when he moved to Fresno, his landlord enforced a no-dogs policy. Kent was thrilled with the thought of interacting with a large dog and helping with Kirby's rehabilitation.

Twice a week, Kent drove his motor bike the two miles from his home to ours. At first, Kent and Kirby took short walks. Once I felt comfortable with Kent taking Kirby out, we added Ivy to the equation. As these walks increased in length and duration, Ivy, the ten-year-old, benefitted as much as three-legged Kirby. The only break in this regimen was when Kirby was hospitalized for his chemo treatments.

As Kirby's stamina improved, we added playtime to Kent's visits. Behind our town house is a small unfenced grass area where the dogs could play fetch. Under Kent's supervision, Kirby and Ivy ran, chased and retrieved. It didn't take long for our fun-loving Goldens to associate Kent's arrival with a good time. At the sound of his motor bike, the dogs frenetically raced around the house in anticipation of his arrival. Ivy greeted him with a toy, while Kirby took to emitting high-pitched squeals of delight.

Another friend, Pat Johnson, was also instrumental in Kirby's rehabilitation. Pat incorporated us into her busy schedule as mother of two school-age children. She drove us twice a week to a nearby park where the dogs could run after tennis balls. At the park Ivy also helped Kirby develop as an agile three-legged athlete. If Kirby retrieved the ball, Ivy would tackle him in an attempt to get it away. Kirby quickly learned to sidestep Ivy, spinning in tight circles to avoid her. This maneuver greatly helped him when he later guided me in restaurants where it was necessary to weave between tightly-packed tables and chairs.

In mid-April, with the chemos behind us and Kirby gaining strength, I began re-asserting the partnership with him as guide. Through consultations with numerous veterinary specialists, I knew Kirby could physically handle his guiding responsibilities. Carefully evaluating Kirby's emotional and mental state of mind, it was clear to me he preferred his role as working partner to that of stay-at-home pet. Kirby, a consummate tail-wagger, showed no stress when working in harness. However, his guiding was less than adequate.

It was obvious he remembered his responsibility of guiding me safely around obstacles and stopping at curbs and steps, but he was extremely hesitant and frequently stopped for no apparent reason. Only after a great deal of coaxing would he resume his guide work. Initially, I attributed this hesitation to the lingering effects of the medical ordeal. What puzzled me was that Kirby worked without hesitation when following Toni and Ivy or when guiding me back to the house.

In early June, I turned to Dr. Ian Dunbar, a renowned veterinary behaviorist we met in Bermuda at the World Congress of Kennel Clubs. Diagnosing the problem as "learned helplessness," he suggested several explicit behavioral modifications to solve the problem.

He explained that, by feeling sorry for Kirby and always allowing Ivy to take the lead, I had unintentionally taken away his initiative. I compounded the problem by coaxing and cajoling Kirby whenever he hesitated. As Ian pointed out, Kirby had come to enjoy all the positive attention he received by not moving forward at the first command. Suggesting I would have to be my own guide dog during the retraining period, Ian told me to carry a white cane to be used when Kirby refused the *forward* command. If Kirby did not move on the first command, I was to drop the harness and leash and, using the white cane to safely move along the sidewalk, leave Kirby where he was. Leaving him behind would, according to Ian, deliver a clear message to Kirby: "I would rather be doing this with you, but if you won't guide me, I'll have to do it without you."

Tapping into a Golden's need to be with his partner, Ian predicted this demonstration of my independence would trigger Kirby's need to resume his role as guide and working partner. It worked! Within a few days, Kirby showed phenomenal improvement in his response to the *forward* command.

Another strategy Ian suggested was to de-emphasize the house. He explained the reason Kirby worked better going back to our house was that it was the source of food and toys. By making the routes interesting and exciting, Kirby's attention would be drawn away from the house. At first, I made the house part of my daily route by going out on short walks, returning home and going out again. To add an element of surprise to the routes, we arranged for friends to meet us at designated spots. On some walks, our friend, Linda Haymond, greeted Kirby with a biscuit in hand and gave us all a ride home. On other occasions, Pat Johnson met us and the reward was a ride to the park and a game of tennis ball.

When KSDS Executive Director Bill Acree and wife Karen, Training Director, came to visit us in late July, Kirby's rehabilitation had progressed so much that they were delightfully astounded. In fact, accompanied by Bill and Karen, we traveled to Berkeley to meet Ian and show off my three-legged wonder dog. He was impressed with Kirby's spirit, as well as his performance as guide. At the end of a demonstration walk, Ian brought tears to our eyes when he said, "That Kirby really has heart!"

In contemplating Kirby's rehabilitation and return to guide work, I was not sure how the public would react. Several people warned me my decision might generate public hostility. To the contrary, I heard, "Your dog sure is loyal!" "He certainly loves you!" "That's one brave dog!" I reveled in these words of support for Kirby, my Miracle Worker.

For the next year Kirby and I made history as Toni and I resumed our careers as lecturers, writers and advocates. In April 1994 we did a ten-day tour in which we lectured at the University of Pennsylvania, Bergh Memorial Hospital of the ASPCA, Angell Memorial Hospital of the Massachusetts SPCA and Tufts University. Whether on the streets of Philadelphia, New York or Boston, Kirby's wagging tail and confident stride drew admiration from all who saw him working. He became a symbol for the disability community, showing that, given the opportunity, a disabled individual can perform the job for which he was trained. The adaptations I needed to make in

order to maintain our partnership were minimal. I changed my
gait, gave Kirby a few extra seconds to line up at the curb and
refurbished his harness so it fit snugly around his shoulders.

Returning from our triumphant tour of the east coast, we
took Kirby in for his six-month checkup. Dr. Larsen was obviously shaken when he told us a tiny spot could be discerned in
Kirby's lungs. From the beginning we realized the cancer could
return, and that's what had happened. Affirmation of Dr. Larsen's
diagnosis was quick in coming.

This time the disease spread so quickly through the Golden
boy's body we could almost see him dying day by day. Within
two weeks he was having trouble walking and we knew the
end was near. Toni and I did a lot of crying and a lot of "what
if-ing" during those days.

As the end drew near, we sent word to all of Kirby's friends,
helpers and admirers that it was time to say goodbye. Many
came to hug and whisper soothing words in his ear. Others
could not face the emotionally charged atmosphere in the
house and did their grieving at a distance.

On the afternoon of the euthanasia, Dr. Larsen came to our
house. As Toni, our friend Carol Palmer and I sat around holding him, Dr. Larsen gently inserted the needle in Kirby's leg and
my beloved partner quietly slipped away. To my astonishment,
this caring veterinarian sat down and delivered a tribute to
Kirby and our partnership. He talked about Kirby's bravery, his
determination, his happy-go-lucky attitude and the impact he
had had on so many people. Finally, Dr. Larsen commended
me for having the foresight to let Kirby resume his career as
guide. His final comments on how privileged he felt to have
known and served us left me feeling considerably more at
peace with my loss.

Grieving is a strange and very personal process. I felt abandoned, I felt cheated, I felt a part of my world had ended, and it had. I began discussing with Toni something I could do to memorialize the life of this wonderful creature who had meant so much to me—and in his disabled state, to many others. We decided to establish a Kirby Memorial Fund for the Newsreel Club, an organization in which approximately 1000 blind members put messages on cassette, ranging from their personal experience with blindness, to songs and puzzles, to assessment of current adaptive technology, to cooking techniques and recipes. Toni and I first heard each other before meeting in person on the Newsreel monthly tapes. Over the years, we have shared our lives and our partnerships with our guide dogs with members of our Newsreel family. This seemed an appropriate place to recognize Kirby. Planning the solicitation of contributions to the fund became a vehicle for putting my grief into a constructive activity. Friends, relatives and Newsreel members sent in their donations, and more than $3000 was raised in Kirby's name.

One of the great tributes to Kirby was his induction into the California Veterinary Medical Associations' Animal Hall of Fame in 1995. Toni and I attended the convention in San Diego where Kirby was recognized at the general session. Dr. James Harris, chair of the state veterinary association's human-animal bond committee, and Dr. Jim Sokalofsky, representative of Waltham, introduced me and my new guide Jake. We accepted the plaque and the check for $500 which are part of the award. We then gave $250 to the Kirby Newsreel Club Memorial Fund and $250 to Guide Dogs of the Desert, Kirby's alma mater.

A WORLD APART

"And God said, Let the earth bring forth the living creature after his kind . . ."

GENESIS 1:24, KJV

$\mathcal{W}$ild animals don't often share people's lives, but they do influence them. Thanks to the work of some extraordinary men and women who have spent years studying the ways of wild animals, most of us now know how to appreciate them. We admire their intelligence and understand their relationships with each other. Perhaps most important, we realize that our well-being is linked to the well-being of all God's creatures.

Smokey Bear

PAUL D. BUCHANAN

$\mathcal{I}$s there an American man, woman, or child—anyone who has camped out sometime in the last 40 years—who would fail to recognize the figure of Smokey Bear? Since 1950, he has addressed Americans from roadside billboards, warning, "Only you can prevent forest fires." On television, he has protected little animals and snuffed out smoldering cigarettes. He has become the symbol of the National Forest Service, of fire prevention, and of camping throughout the United States.

Camping as an organized, popular recreational activity probably began around the turn of the century. Of course, individuals had camped in the wilderness for years before that time. But as the nineteenth century came to a close, organizations such as the Adirondack Mountain Club, the Appalachian Mountain Club, and the Sierra Club came into being. As leisure activities came into greater prominence as the twentieth century progressed, camping became a weekend and holiday pastime for millions of Americans.

Efforts towards forest fire prevention did not begin because of an increased interest in camping. During World War II, the American war effort depended largely upon timber from the California coast and Pacific Northwest. Timber was used to produce cargo ships, gun stocks, and many more military items.

In a move to sabotage some of that war effort, a Japanese sub-marine shelled portions of the California coast, engulfing forest acres and destroying potential timber sources.

In 1942, in an effort to increase public awareness about the danger of such attacks—and of forest fires in general—the United States Forest Service launched a campaign called the Cooperative Forest Fire Prevention Program. The goal was to distribute educational posters among civilians throughout the United States. There was just one problem: the program needed a symbol.

At first the symbol was going to be Bambi the deer, after the 1929 novel that became a Disney movie (which featured a huge forest fire). But the Forest Service decided to look for an original symbol instead, and in 1944, artist Albert Staehles created the first poster of Smokey the Bear. The Forest Service had its symbol; before long, the symbol would come to life.

On May 4, 1942, a huge fire broke out near Capitan Gap in Lincoln National Forest, near the village of Capitan, New Mexico, some 150 miles southeast of Albuquerque. By May 8, more than 17,000 acres of forest had been destroyed by the flames, some of which had been churned by winds reaching speeds of 70 miles per hour.

To fight the blaze, the Department of Fish and Game organized a crew consisting of volunteers and soldiers from nearby Fort Bliss. The crew, led by Fish and Game officer Speed Simmons, barely escaped being engulfed by the flames themselves, by lying flat upon the forest floor and dousing themselves with canteen water. After this terrifying ordeal the crew found their way back to their camp, and headed out the next day, May 9, to grapple anew with the fire.

As they returned to camp at the end of the day, one of the

crewmen spotted a small black bear cub, clinging terror-stricken to the upper trunk of a withered tree. All around were the remains of a charred forest; apparently the cub had wrapped itself around the tree and remained there as the flames roared by. With no mother bear to be found, Simmons sent some of the crew to bring the bear down and take it back to camp. The bear's wounds were covered with salve and bandaged. Crew members fed the cub milk from a bottle and fashioned a bed from a crate.

The next morning, May 10, a Fish and Game officer named Ray Bell took the cub into Santa Fe to see the veterinarian, Dr. E.J. Smith. Smith kept the cub for a week, after which he complained that so many people had come to see the poor baby bear, he could hardly get any work done. Ray Bell eventually took the cub home, where it was cared for by Bell's family.

Before long, the United States Forest Service caught wind of the story of the black bear cub and decided to make the bear the living symbol of its Cooperative Forest Fire Prevention Program. By 1950, the bear cub had been named Smokey, and he had been whisked away to Washington, D.C., where, on June 30, 1950, he officially took up his role as chief spokes-animal for the Forest Service.

Smokey continued to live in Washington until 1976, when he died of old age at the National Zoo. Smokey's body was flown back to the village of Capitan, where it was buried at Smokey Bear State Historic Park. The park, created in the 1950s, featured the Smokey Bear Museum to commemorate Smokey Bear's life, legend, and message. In 1994, the residents of Capitan hosted a celebration of the fiftieth anniversary of Smokey Bear as the symbol of the United States Forest Service.

from FAMOUS ANIMALS OF THE STATES

Punxsutawney Phil

JEAN CRAIGHEAD GEORGE

*E*very year at two in the morning on February 2, fourteen men in tuxedos, black coats and top hats carry a groundhog named Punxsutawney Phil from the cozy zoo near the library to the top of Gobbler's Knob in Punxsutawney, Pennsylvania. He is placed in a hollow stump that is outfitted with a door. Half awake, he curls in a ball and goes back to sleep. The men drink coffee and wait for daybreak.

February 2 is Groundhog Day. If February 2 is bright and clear, there'll be six more weeks of winter; so says the legend the Romans carried to the Teutons, or Germans, and the Germans carried to America. Since the groundhog is a most intelligent and sensible animal, the Pennsylvania Germans reasoned that he, in his wisdom, would see his shadow and go back to sleep for another six weeks of winter. If not, he would stay up, and spring would come early.

In 1871, on February 2, at a dull time of year when the holidays are over and there was little farming to do, a few Punxsutawneyites hied to the woods to test the legend. They found a groundhog and named him Punxsutawney Phil. He answered their question by going back to sleep, and the townspeople feasted and danced. One hundred and twenty-three years later they are still asking Phil about the weather and dancing.

At 7:30 A.M. the president of the Punxsutawney Groundhog Club taps on the stump and awakens Phil. He is irritated. He has been awakened twice this day, and he sees no carrots. He is handed to the president, chittering angrily. The president chitters back. Visitors hold their breath. They are told the man and the groundhog are talking about the weather. Then over the horizon comes the sun, and Phil's shadow falls on the ground.

"Six more weeks of winter," the president carols. The men march down the hill, the band strikes up, and everyone for miles around celebrates Groundhog Day.

Phil is carried home to his zoo. He is not beautiful. He is stout, his tail is short and bushy, his ears are stubby and one is chewed back. He tucks his head into his belly and goes right back to sleep, as he would do in the wild. Groundhogs hibernate in October and awaken in February to locate mates. Ordinarily, they then go back to sleep and get up in March to breed. The young are born in April. Groundhogs devour gardens, crops, flowers and grass. They are easily tamed. These, like Phil, all love to sit on human laps, mow grass all summer and sleep all winter. They are the perfect pet. But no one is really sure how accurate the weather forecasting is, except for Punxsutawneyites. They say their King of the Weather Prophets has never been wrong.

from ANIMALS WHO HAVE WON OUR HEARTS

Cub Life

JOY ADAMSON

---

*F*or many years my home has been in the Northern Frontier
Province of Kenya, that vast stretch of semiarid thornbush, cov-
ering some hundred and twenty thousand square miles, which
extends from Mount Kenya to the Abyssinian border.

Civilization has made little impact on this part of Africa;
there are no settlers; the local tribes live very much as their
forefathers did, and the place abounds in wild life of every
description.

My husband, George, is Senior Game Warden of this huge
territory, and our home is on the southern border of the
Province, near Isiolo, a small township of about thirty Whites,
all of whom are government officials engaged in the task of ad-
ministering the territory.

George has many duties, such as enforcing the Game
Laws, preventing poaching, and dealing with dangerous animals that have molested the tribesmen. His work causes him
to travel over tremendous distances; these journeys we call
safaris. Whenever it is possible I accompany my husband on
such trips, and in this way I have had unique opportunities of
coming to grips with this wild, unchanged land, where life is
tough and nature asserts her own laws.

This story has its beginning on one of these safaris. A

Boran tribesman had been killed by a man-eating lion. It was reported to George that this animal, accompanied by two lionesses, was living in some near-by hills, and so it became his duty to track them down. This was why we were camping far to the north of Isiolo among the Boran tribesmen.

Early on the morning of the first of February, 1956, I found myself in camp alone with Pati, a rock hyrax who had been living with us as a pet for six and a half years. She looked like a marmot or a guinea pig, though zoologists will have it that on account of the bone structure of its feet and teeth, the hyrax is most nearly related to rhinos and elephants.

Pati snuggled her soft fur against my neck and from this safe position watched all that went on. The country around us was dry with outcrops of granite and only sparse vegetation; all the same there were animals to be seen, for there were plenty of gerenuk and other gazelles, creatures that have adapted themselves to these dry conditions and rarely, if ever, drink.

Suddenly I heard the vibrations of a car; this could only mean that George was returning much earlier than expected. Soon our Land Rover broke through the thornbush and stopped near our tents, and I heard George shout: "Joy, where are you? Quick, I have something for you. . . . "

I rushed out with Pati on my shoulder and saw the skin of a lion. But before I could ask about the hunt, George pointed to the back of the car. There were three lion cubs, tiny balls of spotted fur, each trying to hide its face from everything that went on. They were only a few days old and their eyes were still covered with a bluish film. They could hardly crawl; nevertheless they tried to creep away. I took them on my lap to comfort them, while George, who was most distressed, told me what had happened. Toward dawn he and another Game

Warden, Ken, had been guided near to the place where the man-eater was said to lie up. When first light broke they were charged by a lioness who rushed out from behind some rocks. Though they had no wish to kill her, she was very close and the way back was hazardous, so George signalled to Ken to shoot; he hit and wounded her. The lioness disappeared, and when they went forward they found a heavy trail of blood leading upward. Cautiously, step by step, they went over the crest of the hill till they came to a huge flat rock. George climbed onto it to get a better view, while Ken skirted around below. Then he saw Ken peer under the rock, pause, raise his rifle, and fire both barrels. There was a growl; the lioness appeared and came straight at Ken. George could not shoot, for Ken was in his line of fire; fortunately, a Game Scout who was in a more favorable position fired his rifle and caused the animal to swerve; then George was able to kill her. She was a big lioness in the prime of life, her teats swollen with milk. It was only when he saw this that George realized why she had been so angry and faced them so courageously. Then he blamed himself for not having recognized earlier that her behavior showed that she was defending her litter.

Now he ordered a search to be made for the cubs; presently he and Ken heard slight sounds coming out of a crack in the rock face. They put their arms down the crevice as far as they could reach; loud infantile growls and snarls greeted this unsuccessful maneuver. Next they cut a long hooked stick and after a lot of probing managed to drag the cubs out; they could not have been more than two or three days old. They were carried to the car, where the two biggest growled and spat during the whole of the journey back to camp. The third and smallest, however, offered no resistance and seemed quite unconcerned.

Now the three cubs lay in my lap, and how could I resist making a fuss of them?

To my amazement Pati, who was usually very jealous of any rival, soon came to nestle among them, and obviously accepted them as desirable companions. From that day onward, the four became inseparable. During these early days Pati was the biggest of the company and also, being six years old, was very dignified compared with the clumsy little velvet bags who couldn't walk without losing their balance.

It was two days before the cubs accepted their first milk. Until then, whatever trick I tried to make them swallow diluted unsweetened canned milk only resulted in their pulling up their tiny noses and protesting: "ng-ng, ng-ng," very much as we did as children, before we had learned better manners and been taught to say, "No, thank you."

Once they had accepted the milk, they could not get enough of it, and every two hours I had to warm it and clean the flexible rubber tube, which we had taken from the wireless set to serve as a teat until we were able to get a proper baby's bottle. We had sent at once to the nearest African market, which was about fifty miles away, not only for the teat but also for cod-liver oil, glucose, and cases of unsweetened milk and had at the same time sent an S.O.S. to the District Commissioner at Isiolo, about a hundred and fifty miles away, announcing the arrival there within a fortnight of Three Royal Babies, asking him to be good enough to have a comfortable wooden home made in time for our return.

Within a few days the cubs had settled down and were everybody's pets. Pati, their most conscientious self-appointed nanny, remained in charge; she was devoted to them, and never minded being pulled and trodden on by the three fast-growing little bullies. All the cubs were females. Even at this age each had a definite character. The "Big One" had a benevolent superiority and was generous toward the others. The second was a clown, always laughing and spanking her milk bottle with both her front paws as she drank, her eyes closed in bliss. I named her Lustica, which means the "Jolly One."

The third cub was the weakling in size, but the pluckiest in spirit. She pioneered all around, and was always sent by the others to reconnoiter when something looked suspicious to them. I called her Elsa, because she reminded me of someone of that name.

In the natural course of events Elsa would probably have been the throw-out of the pride.[1] The average number of cubs in a litter is four, of which one usually dies soon after birth and another is often too weak to be reared. It is for this reason that one usually sees only two cubs with a lioness. Their mother looks after them till they are two years old. For the first year she provides their food; she regurgitates it, thus making it acceptable to them. During the second year the cubs are allowed to take part in the hunting, but they get severely disciplined if they lose their self-control. Since at this time they are unable to kill on their own, they have to rely for their food on what may be left over from a kill by the full-grown lions of the pride. Often very little remains for them, so they are usually in a bad, scruffy condition at this age. Sometimes they can't bear the hunger; then either they break through the line of gorging adults and

[1]A "pride" is a loose term used to describe the association of more than two lions. It may consist of one or more families living together with some adults, or of a number of adults living together for the purpose of hunting in combination, in contradistinction to a pair of lions or a solitary lion.

are likely to be killed, or they leave the pride, in small groups, and, because they do not yet know how to kill properly, often run into trouble. Nature's law is harsh, and lions have to learn the hard way from the beginning.

The quartet—Pati and the three cubs—spent most of the day in the tent under my camp bed; this evidently seemed to them a safe place and the nearest thing they could find to their natural nursery. They were by nature house-trained and always took great care to reach the sand outside. There were a few accidents during the first days, but afterward, on the rare occasions when a little pool disgraced their home, they miaowed and made comical grimaces of disgust. In every way they were wonderfully clean and had no smell except for a very pleasant one like honey—or was it cod-liver oil? Their tongues were already as rough as sandpaper; as they grew older we could feel them, even through our khaki clothes, when they licked us.

When, after two weeks, we returned to Isiolo, our Royal Babies had a palace awaiting them, everyone came to see them, and they received a royal welcome. They loved Europeans and especially small children but had a marked dislike of Africans; the only exception was a young Somali, called Nuru. He was our garden boy; now we appointed him guardian and lion-keeper in chief. The post pleased him, for it raised his social status; it also meant that when the cubs got tired of romping all over the house and its surroundings and preferred to sleep under some shady bush, he was able to sit near them for long hours, watching to see that no snakes or baboons molested them.

For twelve weeks we kept them on a diet of unsweetened milk mixed with cod-liver oil, glucose, bone-meal, and a little salt. Soon they showed us that they required only three-hourly feeds, and then gradually the intervals became longer.

By now their eyes were fully opened, but they could not yet judge distances and often missed their target. To help them over this difficulty we gave them rubber balls and old inner tubes to play with—the latter were perfect for tug-of-war games. Indeed, anything made of rubber, or that was soft and flexible, fascinated them. They would try to take the inner tube from each other, the attacker rolling sideways onto the possessor, pressing her weight between the end of the tube and its owner. If no success was achieved by this method, the rivals would simply pull with all their might. Then, when the battle had been won, the victor would parade with the trophy in front of the others and provoke an attack. If this invitation was ignored, the rubber would be placed in front of their noses, while the owner pretended to be unaware that it might be stolen from her.

Surprise was the most important element in all their games. They stalked each other—and us—from the earliest age and knew by instinct how to do it properly.

They always attacked from the rear; keeping under cover, they crouched, then crept slowly toward the unsuspecting victim until the final rush was made at flying speed and resulted in the attacker's landing with all her weight on the back of her quarry, throwing it to the ground. When we were the object of such an attack we always pretended to be unaware of what was going on; obligingly we crouched down and looked the other way until the final onslaught took place. This delighted the cubs.

Pati always wanted to be in the game, though, as the cubs were soon three times her size, she took good care to keep out of the way of heavy spankings and to avoid being squashed by her charges. In all other circumstances she retained her authority by sheer character; if the cubs became too aggressive she put them in their places by just turning around and facing them. I admired her spirit, for, small as she was, it needed a lot of courage to convince them of her fearlessness; the more so that her only defenses were her sharp teeth, quick reactions, intelligence, and pluck.

She had come to us when she was newly born, and had entirely adapted her life to ours. Unlike her cousin the tree hyrax, she was not a nocturnal animal, and at night she would sleep around my neck like a fur. She was a vegetarian but had a craving for alcohol, and for the strongest spirits at that; whenever the opportunity arose she would pull the bottle over, extract the cork, and swig the liquor. As this was very bad for Pati's health, not to mention her morale, we took every precaution to prevent any indulgences in whisky or gin.

Her excretory habits were peculiar. Rock hyraxes always use the same place, by preference the edge of a rock; at home Pati invariably perched herself on the rim of the lavatory seat, and thus situated presented a comical sight. On safari where no such refinements were provided for her, she was completely bewildered, so we had eventually to rig up a small lavatory for her.

I never found a flea or a tick on her, so at first I was puzzled by her habit of constantly scratching herself. She had round toenails, like those of a miniature rhino, on her well-padded feet; four toes in front and three behind. On the inner toe of her hind legs there was a claw known as the grooming claw. With this she used to keep her fur sleek and her care for her coat explained her constant scratchings.

Pati had no visible tail; she had a gland along the middle of her spine, which was visible as a white patch in her otherwise

brindled-gray fur. This gland discharged a secretion and the
hair around it used to rise when she became excited by pleasure or alarm. As the cubs grew larger her hair stood up all
too frequently owing to the fear which their playful but rough
antics caused her. Indeed, had she not always been quick to
seek refuge on a window sill, a ladder, or some other high object, she would often have been in danger of being mistaken by
them for a rubber ball. Until the cubs came Pati had always
been number one among our pets. So I was very touched that
she should continue to love the little rascals even though they
diverted our visitors' attention from herself.

As the lions became increasingly aware of their strength,
they tested it on everything they could find. For instance, a
ground sheet, however large, *had* to be dragged about, and
they would set to work in proper feline fashion, placing it
under their bodies and pulling it between their front legs, as in
later life they would drag a kill. Another favorite game was
"king of the castle." A cub would jump onto a potato sack and
keep her attacker at bay until she was suddenly dethroned by
the other sister coming up from behind. The victor was usually
Elsa, who, seeing the other two locked in combat, made the
most of her opportunity.

Our few banana trees were also regarded as delightful toys,
and very soon their luxuriant leaves hung in tattered fringes.
Tree climbing was another favorite game. The little lions were
born acrobats, but often they ventured so high that they could
not turn to come down, and we were obliged to rescue them.

When at dawn Nuru let them out, they shot out of doors
with a whole night's pent-up energy, and this moment could
be compared to the start of a greyhound race. On one such oc-
casion they spotted a tent in which two men who had come to

visit us were staying. Within five minutes it was a wreck and we were awakened by the cries of our guests who were vainly trying to rescue their belongings, while the cubs, wild with excitement, dived into the wreckage and reappeared with a variety of trophies—slippers, pajamas, shreds of mosquito netting. We had to enforce discipline that time with a small stick.

Putting them to bed was also no mean task. Imagine three very naughty little girls, who like all children hated bedtime, but who could run twice as fast as those who were in charge of them and had the added advantage of being able to see in the dark.

We were often obliged to resort to subterfuge. One very successful trick was to tie an old bag to a length of rope and drag it steadily toward and then into the pen; usually they could not resist chasing it.

Outdoor games were all very well, but the cubs also developed a fancy for books and cushions. So, to save our library and other possessions, we were eventually obliged to ban them from the house; to effect this we made a shoulder-high door of strong wire on a wooden frame and placed it across the entrance to the veranda. The cubs resented it very much, so to compensate them for their lost playground we hung a tire from a tree, and this proved to be grand for chewing and also as a swing. Another toy we gave them was an empty wooden honey barrel which made a resounding boom when it was pushed. But best of all was a hessian bag. We filled it with old inner tubes and tied it to a branch, from which it dangled invitingly. It had another rope attached to it, and when the cubs hung on to the bag we pulled and swung them high up into the air; the more we laughed the better they enjoyed the game.

Yet none of these toys caused them to forget that there was

at all times a barrier in front of the veranda, and they often came and rubbed their soft noses against the wire.

Late one afternoon some friends had arrived for a sundowner. Intrigued by the sounds of merriment inside, the cubs soon turned up, but that evening they behaved in a disciplined fashion; there was no nose-rubbing against the wire; all three kept a foot away from it. This exemplary conduct aroused my suspicion, so I got up to investigate its cause. To my horror, I saw a large red spitting cobra between the cubs and the door. In spite of the presence of three lions on one side and of ourselves on the other, it wriggled determinedly across the veranda steps, and by the time we had fetched a shotgun it had disappeared.

No barricades, cobras, or prohibitions made Lustica give up her intention of entering the house; repeatedly she tried all the doors. Pressing a handle proved easy enough; even turning a knob could be done; only when we quickly fitted bolts all around was she defeated, and even so I once caught her trying to push the bolt aside with her teeth. Thwarted in her purpose, she had her revenge upon us, for about this time she tore the laundry off the clothesline and galloped off into the bush with it.

When the cubs were three months old they had teeth big enough to make it possible for them to eat meat. So now I gave them raw minced meat, which was the best we could do to imitate their mother's regurgitated food. For several days they refused to touch it and pulled grimaces of disgust. Then Lustica made the experiment, and found it to her taste. The others took courage from her, and soon there was a fight at every meal. This meant that poor Elsa, who was still weaker than the others, had little chance of getting her fair share, so I kept the tidbits for her and used to take her on to my lap for her meals. She loved this; rolling her head from side to side and closing her eyes, she showed how happy she was. At these times she would suck my thumbs and massage my thighs with her front paws as though she were kneading her mother's belly in order to get more milk. It was during these hours that the bond between us developed. We combined playing with feeding, and my days were happily spent with these charming creatures.

They were lazy by nature and it needed a lot of persuasion to get them to move from a comfortable position. Even the most desirable marrow bone was not worth the effort of getting up, and they would roll into position to get at it by the easiest way. But best of all they liked me to hold their bone for them while they lay on their backs, paws in the air, and sucked at it.

When the cubs went into the bush they often had adventures. One morning I was following them, for I had given them a worming powder and wished to see the result. I saw them a little way off asleep. Suddenly I noticed a stream of black soldier ants approaching them. Indeed, some were already climbing up their bodies. Knowing how fiercely these ants will attack anything that lies in their path and how powerful their mandibles are, I was just about to wake up the cubs when the ants changed their direction.

Soon afterwards five donkeys approached and the cubs woke up. This was the first time they had seen such big animals, and they certainly showed the proverbial courage of a lion, for they all charged simultaneously. This put them into such good heart that when, a few days later, our forty pack donkeys and mules came near the house, the three little lions fearlessly put the whole cavalcade to flight.

At five months they were in splendid condition and getting

stronger every day. They were quite free except at night, when they slept in an enclosure of rock and sand which led off from their wooden shelter. This was a necessary precaution, for wild lions, hyenas, jackals, and elephants frequently roam around our house, and any of these might have killed them.

The more we grew to know the cubs the more we loved them, so it was hard to accept the fact that we could not keep forever three fast-growing lions. Regretfully we decided that two must go and that it would be better that the two big ones, who were always together and less dependent on us than Elsa, should be the ones to leave. Our African servants agreed with our choice; when asked their opinion they unanimously chose the smallest. Perhaps they were influenced by visions of the future and thought: "If there must be a lion in the household, then let it be as small as possible."

As to Elsa, we felt that if she had only ourselves as friends she would be easy to train, not only for life at Isiolo but also as a travelling companion on our safaris.

As a home for Lustica and the Big One, we chose the Rotterdam-Blydorp Zoo and made arrangements for them to make the journey by air.

Since they would have to leave from the Nairobi airfield, which was one hundred and eighty miles away, we decided to get them accustomed to motoring, and took them for short daily trips in my one-and-a-half-ton truck, which had a wired box body. We also began to feed them in it, so that they might get used to it and consider it as one of their play pens.

On the last day we padded the car with soft sand-bags.

When we drove off, Elsa ran a short way down the drive and then stood with the most mournful expression in her eyes watching the car in which her two sisters were disappearing.

I travelled in the back with the cubs and had armed myself with a small first-aid kit fully expecting to be scratched during the long journey. However, my medical precautions were put to shame, for, after an hour of restlessness, the cubs lay on the bags beside me, embracing me with their paws. We travelled like this for eleven hours, delayed by two blow-outs. The lions could not have been more trusting. When we reached Nairobi they looked at me with their large eyes, puzzled to know what to make of all the strange noises and smells. Then the plane carried them off forever from their native land.

After a few days we received a cable announcing the safe arrival of our cubs in Holland. When I visited them, about three years later, they accepted me as a friendly person and allowed me to stroke them, but they did not recognize me. They live in splendid conditions and, on the whole, I was glad to know that almost certainly they had no recollection of a freer life.

from BORN FREE

Simo:
The Healing Dolphin

JOHN G. SUTTON

*I*magine living your life alone in a dark room, unable to love or be loved. Depression is like that.

Bill Bowell was suffering badly. The doctors had tried everything to cure him—tablets, injections, hospital, hypnosis. Bill's family loved him dearly. His five children were desperate to bring back the man they were proud to call Dad. His wife Edna refused to give in. Every day she and the children made some attempt to reach into her husband's darkness. But no matter what they tried, Bill remained a prisoner of clinical depression.

In the summer of 1986, Edna decided to take the family away on holiday. For almost twelve years Bill had been a sick man, struggling against the mental pain that crippled him as surely as if he had been bound. Perhaps some sea air might release him.

Edna drove the family up from Oxford to Wales, to the Pembrokeshire coastal village of Solva, near St. David's. They had hired an old stone cottage for a week. The fresh air would do all of them good and there is always plenty of that on the Pembrokeshire coast.

On the first night of the holiday Mrs. Bowell suggested they all go into the village and visit the local pub, the Harbour Hotel. Bill didn't mind. He never minded anything: nothing mattered to him, nothing at all.

Inside the hotel, Susan, the eldest daughter, ordered the drinks while Edna settled Bill in a corner seat. Looking around, she saw a notice board and went up to it. There was a hand-written notice announcing a meeting that night at a nearby hall. A talk and film show would be given by a Dr. Dobbs. The subject was dolphins.

Edna thought it might be an idea to go along to the lecture. When she asked Bill if he wanted to go, he replied, "Yes, please." By ordinary standards this is not a tremendous re-sponse, but Bill hardly ever spoke and was not usually keen enough even to say please.

The film showed dolphins swimming freely in the sea. After-ward Dr. Dobbs gave a short talk. He said he was in Solva to make another film and conduct research.

When Dr. Dobbs talked about dolphins, it was as if he were speaking directly to Bill. He seemed to be offering a chance for Bill to climb out of his darkness into the light. The pictures of those dolphins swimming had created a weird feeling deep inside him.

After the talk had ended, Bill did something he hadn't done in years: he went up and spoke to a stranger. Dr. Dobbs lis-tened politely, but told Bill that he was a very busy man. But Bill's daughter Karen was not going to leave it there. She fol-lowed Dr. Dobbs to the door and asked him to help her father. She told him how desperate the family were to bring back to life the man they all loved. Dr. Dobbs must have been im-pressed by her determination, because he agreed to take Bill out to see the dolphins. He told Karen that if she and the family could get Bill Bowell onto the harbor wall at ten o'clock the next morning, he could join that day's crew on the boat going out into St. Bride's Bay to meet a dolphin called Simo.

The following day, at exactly 10 A.M., Dr. Dobbs welcomed Bill on board his boat. He had brought with him a flask of hot coffee and some sandwiches prepared by Karen and Susan. They were determined that their dad was not going to miss this chance at experiencing something new. They hoped it might give Bill back the will to live that he had lost so many years ago.

About half an hour out into St. Bride's Bay, round Ramsey Island and past St. David's Head, the skipper pointed the boat into a secluded bay. As the boat coasted about fifty yards out from the rugged shoreline, Bill saw a fin cutting through the green water. "That's Simo," said Dr. Dobbs.

Bill's heart beat faster as he watched the dolphin approach the boat. Closer and closer it came; he could see the outline of the animal now, steel grey in the pale sea lit by the morning sunlight, streaking gracefully through the waves.

Suddenly Simo the dolphin burst through the foam and, swishing his powerful tail, stood straight up alongside the boat right next to Bill Bowell. From the moment Bill looked into Simo's eyes, he was transfixed. Without thinking, he reached forward and touched the dolphin's head. A thought jumped into his mind: "We need each other." How long he was leaning forward and stroking the dolphin, Bill doesn't know. Time stood still. All that mattered was the thought that the dolphin loved and needed him.

Dr. Dobbs, watching very carefully, had seen the joy spreading through Bill Bowell as, for the first time in twelve years, the man smiled. "He says we need each other," Bill said. "Simo needs me." There were tears of pure happiness running down his face. In that brief encounter with the dolphin, Bill had begun to unlock the door of his personal prison cell. Simo had given him the key, a key called love.

Quickly Dr. Dobbs dressed Bill Bowell in a diver's wet suit. It didn't fit very well, because Bill had taken no exercise at all during his long illness, but they got it on him. Then Dr. Dobbs helped Bill slip over the side of the boat to swim with Simo the dolphin.

It was the first time he had been in the sea for years. Perhaps Simo sensed this, for within seconds he was swimming alongside Bill and gently pushing him up, keeping him afloat with his nose.

As Bill Bowell swam with Simo, he began to feel that the dolphin was trying to tell him something very important. When he looked into Simo's eyes, the message registered in his mind. The dolphin was saying, "I need you! Please come and share my mysterious world." The shock made Bill almost cry out loud. He became lost in that beautiful creature's magical company, swam like an athlete and forgot completely that he was a sick man.

"Mr. Bowell! Come in, Mr. Bowell!"

Bill was surprised to hear himself summoned back. It only seemed like a few minutes that he had been with Simo, and the dolphin needed him. But in fact Bill had been swimming with Simo for almost an hour. It took quite a bit of persuading to get him back on board, because he was so enthralled by the dolphin.

Dr. Dobbs was delighted with Bill's response to swimming with Simo and invited him along on the following and final day of his dolphin observations. Once again, Bill was transformed by that magnificent creature. So changed was he that Dr. Dobbs asked the boat owner if he would consider taking Bill out himself after Dr. Dobbs and the camera team had left. The man at once agreed; he could see how much the dolphin meant to Bill.

Each morning for the rest of the week's holiday, the boatman met Bill Bowell at the harbor wall and took him out to swim with Simo the dolphin. Bill believes that Simo saved his life, because by the end of the seven days he had almost shaken off his long illness.

In the months after Bill's meeting with Dr. Dobbs, they kept in contact. The doctor wanted to assess the long-term effect that swimming with the dolphin might have. Bill's wife and all his children often answered Dr. Dobbs's calls with the marvellous news that Bill was, almost miraculously, healed. Not that this surprised the good doctor. He had always thought that dolphins could have a positive effect on human beings suffering from clinical depression. Now he had the living proof: Bill Bowell was cured.

Since that first meeting with Simo, Bill has swum with other dolphins. Dr. Dobbs took him to Ireland to meet a very beautiful dolphin called Funghie, who immediately befriended Bill. Together they swam in the seas around the Irish coast, rubbing noses, diving, dancing in the cool green waves, and, Bill felt, sharing the joy of just being alive together.

Bill says that there is an energy force that seems to enter his body as he swims with dolphins. This force invigorates him, fills him with a delight in living that had been locked away all those long, dark years when he was ill. Now Bill only has to see a dolphin to feel better. But he just can't stand to watch captive dolphins, not after swimming with them in the wild. Even the old films of Flipper are instantly switched off in the Bowell household.

Today Bill Bowell is living testimony to the healing powers of dolphins. Specialist physicians from all over the world have attended, by invitation of Dr. Dobbs, to watch Bill Bowell and the dolphins together. The pioneering work of Dr. Dobbs and the example of Mr. Bowell did much to bring about the international appreciation of the healing powers of dolphins. Since then, many unhappy people have enjoyed dolphin cures.

from ANIMALS MAKE YOU FEEL BETTER

Koko

PAUL D. BUCHANAN

The relationship that has historically existed between humans and animals is less an actual relationship than a coexistence. Obviously, animals and humans have interacted and affected each other since the dawn of time, but without the one element that is essential for a relationship: the mutual exchange of ideas that constitutes real communication. Certainly, humans have long fantasized about the ability to communicate with animals. But for the most part, human beings have simply given orders, to which animals have responded in a positive or negative fashion. So much for communication, and so much for a relationship.

Then along came a western lowland gorilla named Koko. Koko was born on July 4, 1971, at the San Francisco Zoo, the offspring of Jackie and Bwana. Her formal name was Hanabiko, which is Japanese for "fireworks child," but everyone called her Koko. Life for Koko would have been pretty much the same as for every other gorilla raised in captivity, were it not for a Stanford University graduate student of developmental psychology named Francine Patterson. Patterson's fascination with the idea of communicating with animals spearheaded what came to be known as the Koko Project. Since 1972, Dr. Patterson and Koko have been learning to communicate with one an-

other using American Sign Language. Under Patterson's tute-
lage, Koko has learned to communicate in rhyme, to tell jokes,
even to lie.

When Patterson met Koko, the gorilla had been ill with
shigella enteritis. She had become severely malnourished and
dehydrated and had to be isolated from her mother and the
other gorillas. This isolation may have been key to Patterson's
selection of Koko, since Koko would have already been used to
separation from the other gorillas, and development away
from the gorilla community would not be as traumatic for her
as it might for other gorilla children.

Although Patterson had yet to be granted permission to
work with the gorilla, she began to visit Koko in recovery every
day. At first, Koko was extremely wary of Patterson, and even
bit her when she tried to pick Koko up. Slowly but surely, however, Koko came to trust Patterson, and as they spent more
time together, an intimate bond began to form. This bond became integral to the success of Project Koko.

American Sign Language does not rely on finger-spelling of
words, but rather on gestures that convey complete ideas. For
example, "drink" is conveyed with a clenched fist, thumb extended and brought up to the lips. Koko's venture into American Sign Language began with the signs for "drink," "food,"
and "more." Patterson used these signs whenever Koko ate,
and she instructed the zoo assistants who worked in Koko's
nursery to use the signs as well. Whenever Koko was presented
with food, it was accompanied by the ASL sign for food; whenever she was given drink, the "drink" sign was shown with it;
when Koko was given more food, the assistants signed "more."

This repetition continued for about a month. Then, one
morning, as Patterson was preparing Koko's snack, the gorilla

formed the sign for "food" with her hands. As Patterson watched in amazement, Koko made the sign again. Patterson was ecstatic, and the gorilla, apparently sharing in her friend's excitement, joy, and sense of accomplishment, put a bucket on her head and began running happily about the room. The human and the gorilla had crossed an important bridge: They had learned to communicate an idea.

Patterson's attempts to communicate with a gorilla at first met with much skepticism from colleagues. Most of them assumed that a chimpanzee would be a better choice for such a project. Gorillas, in comparison to chimpanzees, were considered dim-witted, slow, and dangerous, because of their enormous strength and relatively unknown character. The gorilla's shy, retiring ways were evidently mistaken for a lack of intelligence, while the chimpanzee's gregarious nature—it often seems to enjoy the company of humans—was accepted as a sign of superior intellect.

Over the years, however, Koko's intelligence and resourcefulness have made themselves obvious. At the age of four years, the gorilla had a vocabulary of more than 161 words, and by five years it had passed 350 words. Today her vocabulary is well over 600 words. But more important than Koko's simple accumulation of words has been her ability to communicate about the world from the gorilla's point of view.

For example, during one conversation about death, Koko was asked where gorillas go when they die. Koko responded by signing, "Comfortable hole bye," exhibiting none of the trepidation which often accompanies a human conversation about death. When asked where baby gorillas come from, Koko signed her own name; when asked where in Koko babies come from, Koko pointed to her abdomen. Other conversations have included such topics as gorilla fears, the differences and similarities between humans and gorillas, and the use of sign language itself.

In 1974, Patterson, Koko, and Dr. Ronald Cohn (document-ing photographer for Project Koko) moved to a trailer and compound at Stanford University, where Project Koko was continued. In 1979, they all moved to a farm in Woodside, some ten miles north of Stanford. Along the way a male gorilla named Michael was acquired as a companion to Koko. In 1984, Koko was given a pet, a cat she named "All Ball." And of course, the breakthrough work of Koko and Patterson has been the focus of worldwide media attention. *Science, Reader's Digest,* and *National Geographic* have all featured articles on their compelling story, as have the television and radio news media throughout the world.

Project Koko continues in the hills of Woodside, California, to this day. Although there have been other communica-tion projects with apes—most notably, the work of Allan and Beatrice Gardner with a female chimpanzee named Washoe, which provided much inspiration for Dr. Patterson's work— Project Koko is the longest ongoing study of language capabil-ities in apes. As the project continues to unfold, the relationship of Dr. Patterson and Koko continues to grow—as a real rela-tionship, based on their appreciation for one another's point of view.

from FAMOUS ANIMALS OF THE STATES

MOMENTS IN HISTORY

"Wherever our paths have led, the tracks
of animals have been alongside them."

ROBERT MERRIWEATHER

$\mathcal{I}$t's exciting to look at history through the eyes of animals—and they were there whenever anything important happened. They were with us when we discovered new lands and built nations. They helped us turn a wilderness into a home. They made it possible for us to get from one place to another and to keep in touch with those we left behind. They were our companions, our defenders, our teachers, and in their simple way they were reminders that God was always with us.

And they still are.

The Pacing
White Mustang

JEAN CRAIGHEAD GEORGE

In the days when herds of buffalo still roamed the Great Plains, the Pacing White Mustang lived in wild splendor somewhere "out west." As beautiful as fresh mountain snow, he sped like a tornado across the prairie and commanded his herd like a general. The Osage Indians said he was a ghost. Cowboys said he was a mirage. Stories were written about his strength and beauty, and prizes were offered for his capture. But no one could rope him.

The White Mustang's speed was legendary. According to the few who had glimpsed him, he moved his front and back legs simultaneously—first on one side and then on the other. This dynamic gait is called "pacing." (Most horses put forward the front right with back left legs, then the front left with the back right.) Running across the Plains in his own unique way, the white pacer fairly flew.

In 1832, famous author Washington Irving was lucky enough to see the magnificent white stallion while on a tour of the prairies with the Commissioner of Indian Affairs. And a few years later, an army general and one of his captains also encountered him. The men were awakened one night by the sounds of battle between wild horses and wolves. At daylight, they rode out to catch the horses for the army. About a mile downstream they came upon the howling wolves and a herd of about 150 horses. Rising above them all, flailing his feet as he commanded, was the Pacing White Mustang. He had formed the mares in a circle facing inward so they could kick the enemy with their hoofs. Protected inside the circle were the colts and yearlings. What was most extraordinary was that the white mustang ruled the other stallions. Stallions usually fight each other, but at the command of the white pacer they charged the wolves who were attacking the herd.

As soon as the wolves scented the men, they ran off, and the soldiers went after the horses. The Pacing White Mustang instantly signaled his stallions. They turned, pawed the ground in front of the mares, and neighed. The mares opened their circle. The colts and yearlings ran out and the stallions led them off. The mares followed the colts.

The white stallion brought up the rear and took on the men alone. He would let a rider come to within twenty yards of him, then pull swiftly away, fall back, and let another horseman approach. In this manner he held off the horse raiders until his herd was out of sight. Then he vanished. Even the disappointed general had to admit that he, and all the others who had tried but failed to capture the white stallion, had been outsmarted by a remarkable horse.

from INCREDIBLE ANIMAL ADVENTURES

A Race With Death

TIM JONES

$\mathcal{W}$herever there are races, there are arguments. Teenagers argue Fords and Chevys. Horsemen argue thoroughbreds and quarter horses. In Nome, Alaska, arguments surrounded the All-Alaska Sweepstakes, a sled dog race in the early 1900s in which various companies owned the dog teams and hired the drivers. Owners of the popular malemute regularly argued with fans of the Siberian husky, recently imported from Siberia.

One proponent of the Siberian was Leonhard Seppala. A Norwegian by birth, Seppala arrived in Nome to prospect for gold in 1901. According to his biography, he quickly tired of that and, having learned to drive dogs, hired his services to the Hammon Consolidated Gold Fields Company.

During his time in Nome, Seppala trained and drove dogs for the mining company and entered many of the races sponsored by the Nome Kennel Club. His Siberians were consistent champions. But his greatest race was not against other dog teams, but against time and weather and a deadly epidemic of diphtheria that threatened the children of Nome in January of 1925.

Diphtheria was diagnosed in several children by Nome's Dr. Curtis Welch that month. Nome desperately needed the serum that would save the children, but airplanes couldn't fly through the rough weather to reach the Bering Sea city. So a doctor in Anchorage organized a sled dog relay to bring the medicine from the closest railroad stop, in Nenana, 650 miles across Alaska to Nome.

The city fathers sent Seppala to meet the medicine at the village of Nulato on the Yukon River, a distance of more than 300 miles. Seppala left Nome with twenty dogs, planning to leave a few in villages along the way to rest so he could pick them back up, refreshed, for the trip back. In front of the team was his favorite lead dog, a Siberian named Togo who Seppala had raised and trained himself.

With Togo in lead, Seppala pushed his way along the south coast of the Seward Peninsula toward Unalakleet, where there was a portage through the mountains to the Interior. At Isaac's Point, Seppala faced a choice. He could set out across the dangerous sea ice on Norton Sound, or he could take the safer but longer trail around the east end of the sound. He'd heard reports that the pack ice had been moving and was unstable, but he set out across the ice despite the hazard.

Trusting his dogs to lead him around any open water, Seppala almost reached the far shore of the sound when his dogs stopped. He watched them raise their ears and reach for scent with their noses, a clear indication that other dogs were nearby. Then he heard a call. He let the dogs move toward whatever it was they were smelling, and together they came upon another dog team.

It was driven by musher Henry Ivanoff, from the Eskimo village of Unalakleet. Ivanoff explained that he was the last in a chain of more than twenty mushers who had been recruited to relay the serum through the −50° and −60° F temperatures of the Interior and get it into Seppala's hands. If Seppala would take the serum back toward Nome, he would soon meet up with other mushers from Nome who would carry it the rest of the way.

Ivanoff handed the medicine over to Seppala, who immediately packed it into the sled and turned back toward Nome. This time he attempted an even shorter route, going straight northwest from Cape Denbeigh to Cape Darby. On this more treacherous trail his dogs fell through thin ice, and Seppala spent several terror-filled moments bringing them back onto a solid surface. The team passed Cape Darby and raced for the village of Golovin.

There he gave the serum to Charlie Olson, who headed west toward Nome. About thirty miles down the trail, Olson reached the outpost at Bluff where Gunnar Kaasen was waiting. Like Seppala, Kaasen worked for the Hammon Company, and many of the dogs he drove had been trained by Seppala, including a malamute leader named Balto. With his fresh team and Balto in the lead, Kaasen raced toward Safety, an outpost just twenty-two miles east of Nome. There Kaasen was supposed to meet one last dog team that would take the serum to town.

Instead, Kaasen passed Safety and headed right for Nome. He later was quoted in the *New York Times* as saying that the dogs felt good and were making good time, so he thought he'd just go on. Another report claimed that Kaasen, fighting a blinding storm, missed Safety accidentally. For whatever reason, Kaasen pushed on into a growing blizzard. Along that part of the coast, storms often send winds howling through the valleys, blasting travelers with the driving snow. Kaasen, Balto, and the rest of the dogs battled that storm for hours, then triumphantly emerged from it on Nome's Front Street to deliver the serum.

The *New York Times,* receiving reports by telegraph first from Nome, then from Anchorage and Fairbanks, had followed the "race against death" every day for more than a week. When the crisis was finally over, it was only natural for the paper to make a hero out of the lead dog who had brought the serum to Nome. Balto became a hero worldwide, a symbol of strength and devotion and endurance, the dog who saved Nome.

Balto became a hero to everyone, except perhaps his owner and trainer. Leonhard Seppala maintained to his death that the true hero of the serum run was Togo, who had led Seppala's team almost 180 miles on very little rest, and who had saved the team time and time again on the moving ice of Norton Sound.

Who was the greater hero? Balto, with his statue in New York's Central Park, or Togo, the driver's own choice? Like most racing arguments, this one probably will never be resolved. Nor does it matter. Both dogs did their part according to their abilities. If Balto has become a symbol of that race against death, he stands for all the dogs who participated, all of the heroes who raced to save the children of Nome.

from DOG HEROES

Ready to Gallop

JOHN FLEISCHMAN

The taxidermist set Winchester's head slightly lifted, ears cocked and a forehoof poised—the picture of the old campaigner listening for the rumble of a distant fight. Winchester is magnificent; 16 hands high, jet black and wearing a general's saddle trappings, he stands in the Hall of Armed Forces History at the Smithsonian's National Museum of American History.

He was a big gelding who caught the eye of a Union colonel, a swarthy Irishman from rural Ohio with long arms, short legs and an unforgettable bullet-shaped head. Phil Sheridan named the horse Rienzi, after the Mississippi town in which Sheridan's troops had been encamped, and rode him over the next three years through 45 engagements including 19 pitched battles and two cavalry raids. Along the way, Rienzi became so famous that he was briefly a factor in the Presidential election of 1864 and a staple of patriotic entertainment for veterans, Republicans and schoolchildren for a half-century.

A poem, "Sheridan's Ride," was written by a minor painter and versifier named Thomas Buchanan Read. It was used shamelessly to promote the Northern war effort. Whatever its literary flaws, Read's poem captured one image indelibly—a powerful horse carrying a determined man into battle.

They must have been a sight, the horse who measured

5 feet 8 at the shoulder and his master who stood 5 feet 5 in his boots. Soldiers snickered that "Little Phil" shinnied up his saber to Rienzi's saddle, but there were no snickers on October 19, 1864, when horse and rider appeared through the smoke at Cedar Creek to stem certain defeat in the Shenandoah Valley. Sheridan's army had been surprised at dawn and driven from their camp by Jubal Early's Confederate veterans. Returning from Washington, Sheridan had spent the night up the valley in Winchester and awoke to distant gunfire. The Confederate assault had smashed the Union left, sending survivors pelting up the valley turnpike toward Winchester. The Union center made a brief stand, then fell back, nervously awaiting Early's next charge.

Sheridan and Rienzi, meanwhile, were heading south from Winchester, toward the sound of the guns. After cresting a ridge, Sheridan recalled, "there burst upon our view the appalling spectacle of a panic-stricken army . . . throngs of unhurt but utterly demoralized [men] and baggage wagons by the score, all pressing to the rear. . . . "

Sheridan dashed forward, waving his hat so the troops would see him. Some cheered and found new heart. Some kept running. But the rolling sound of cheering followed Sheridan and the well-lathered Rienzi as the general rode up to a rise where a few rattled Union commanders had gathered.

He quickly took verbal reports. Then wheeling Rienzi, he jumped a rail barricade, rode forward and turned to face the men behind him. "Men, by God, we'll whip them yet," he bellowed. "We'll sleep in our old camps tonight." The troops jumped forward, roaring. A private who saw Sheridan ride into sight remembered thinking, "No more doubt or chance for doubt existed; we were safe, and every man knew it."

Twelve days later in Cincinnati, Tom Read was talking with James Murdoch, a matinee idol scheduled to read patriotic verse at a war benefit that evening. Read's brother-in-law walked in, carrying *Harper's Weekly* with a battlefield sketch by Thomas Nast of Sheridan riding Rienzi toward Cedar Creek. "Buck, there's a poem in that picture," he said. . . .

Read bristled, "Do you suppose I can write a poem to order?" Nonetheless he shut himself in his study and, by noon, called for his wife to copy "Sheridan's Ride" out fair.

That night, Murdoch uncorked the verse that would gallop across a nation and through countless poetry collections for children yet unborn. To keep up suspense, at the end of each verse, Sheridan was closer to the battle: "Up from the South at break of day, / Bringing to Winchester fresh dismay, / The affrighted air with a shudder bore, / The terrible grumble and rumble and roar, / Telling the battle was on once more, / And Sheridan twenty miles away."

"Sheridan's Ride" was a timely sensation. The election of 1864 had been hanging in the balance. People were tired of the war. In Chicago, the "Peace" Democrats had put up George B. McClellan, hoping the onetime military figure with an aversion to battle would appeal to an electorate that also seemed to be sick of Abraham Lincoln.

Only Sheridan's victories in the Shenandoah looked undimmed in Republican war politics. In August, Grant ordered Sheridan to smash Early's army and make sure the Shenandoah never harbored another rebel force. By early October, Sheridan had already whipped Early twice, and his forces were burning the valley's crops. "A crow," he reported, "would have had to carry its rations if it had flown across the valley."

But Early's masterful attack at Cedar Creek nearly unseated Sheridan—and with him, Lincoln. When Rienzi delivered Sheridan in the nick of time, the Republican Party was eternally grateful. Read made the debt explicit: "Here is the steed that saved the day / By carrying Sheridan into the fight / From Winchester—twenty miles away!"

"Widely read and recited, the piece made a fine recruiting and electioneering appeal," according to Civil War historian Shelby Foote. On Election Day, Horace Greeley's influential *New York Tribune* called it "a magnificent lyric" and ran the seven stanzas of "Sheridan's Ride" on page one. It is impossible to know how many votes Read's verses delivered to Lincoln, but in New York, every vote was critical. Lincoln carried the state by fewer than 7,000 votes and Connecticut by 2,000.

Lincoln's re-election was safe, but the war still had five fearful months to run. Now Rienzi got fully "stretched out," as newspapers reprinted Read's poem. "The thing they seem to like best about it," said Sheridan, "is the horse." He graciously acknowledged his debt in a letter to Read. "Your genius has put us into the same boat for a long journey, and we must try and take along the black horse."

Read had yet to cash in on his poem; the newspapers, the Republicans and the platform elocutionists had helped themselves. Read felt that only a painted version of "Sheridan's Ride" by his hand would yield real return. In 1865 Sheridan, posted to New Orleans to keep a baleful eye on French moves in Mexico, agreed to pose with Rienzi.

Read spent a month in New Orleans doing preliminary sketches. Then he finished painting his self-proclaimed masterpiece in Italy. "There may be poets who would write a better poem than 'Sheridan's Ride,'" he wrote, "but could the same man paint a better picture? There may be painters who could produce a better picture, but could the same artist write a better poem?"

Read launched into plans to issue the painting as a color lithograph suitable for framing.

But he did not have long to enjoy his profits. Heading home in 1872, a cold he caught on the Liverpool docks turned to pneumonia at sea. In New York a week later, he died at age 50.

Rienzi was next, although by then Sheridan had officially renamed him Winchester. He had carried the general to Appomatox Court House, there to wait outside, nervously twitching his tail as always, while, as Sheridan looked on, Lee and Grant brought the Civil War to a close.

When the old war-horse died in 1878, he was stuffed (or "mounted" as taxidermists insist) and presented to the military museum on Governor's Island in New York Harbor.

Ten years later, Sheridan, too, was dead, at 57. He was only 33 at Cedar Creek, and a long Army career took him from enforcing Reconstruction in the South to observing the Franco-Prussian War to fighting the Indian Wars on the Great Plains. He wound up in 1888 as Commander in Chief of the Army.

Adverse critical reaction to "Sheridan's Ride" eventually set in. Picky historians kept pointing out that Sheridan's route from Winchester to Cedar Creek was more like 12 miles than Read's 20. They claimed that Sheridan couldn't have ridden hell-for-leather along a road choked with a defeated army. But the ride was for real, and Rienzi/Winchester was no fake.

from SMITHSONIAN

Scannon, More Than a Mascot

JEAN CRAIGHEAD GEORGE

---

*B*red for the noble purpose of rescuing people at sea, Scannon, a large, lovable Newfoundland dog, defied his heredity to become a food gatherer, a retriever, a bear dog and a collector of biological specimens.

He belonged to Meriwether Lewis, captain of the Lewis and Clark Expedition sent out by President Thomas Jefferson in May 1804. The expedition would determine if the Missouri and Columbia rivers could provide a water route across North America to the rich Northwest. Scannon, mascot of the expedition, sensed his job was more than looking handsome. He caught squirrels for food, drowned a wolf and was seriously wounded by the beaver he caught for Lewis's collection of wildlife. The collection had been requested by President Jefferson.

The expedition was far up the Missouri River when Scannon's wounds were healed. Migrating geese settled down on the river by the thousands. Scannon jumped into the water and caught one after another for the table. Game was not always easy to come by, and the crew rewarded Scannon's spectacular efforts with high praise. The attention was so heady that the big dog was inspired to greater feats. He drove human-killing grizzly bears out of camp in the Yellowstone River region and took on a bull buffalo that thundered across the Missouri and into the midst of the sleeping crew on the ground. Barking and herding like a sheepdog, he maneuvered the bull around men in sleeping bags and back across the Missouri River.

Calling on the talents of all breeds of dogs, Scannon rode in boats, tracked, retrieved, killed snakes, dug into holes to collect what lived there, and arrived with his master in good health at the Pacific Coast on January 6, 1806. There Scannon hunted elk and collected wildlife until it was time to start back to St. Louis in March.

Still performing his self-imposed duties, Scannon arrived in St. Louis on September 23, 1806, together with all the men but one, who had died of appendicitis. As Scannon jumped ashore, he completed a journey that some historians consider the most successful and intelligent expedition in history. Eventually the route would bind the east and the west together as the United States of America.

Scannon knew nothing of this. He and his master were home.

from ANIMALS WHO HAVE WON OUR HEARTS

A Beautiful Stranger

MICHAEL ALLIN

Zarafa entered Lyon on schedule on Tuesday, June 5, 1827. That same day, Athens fell to the Turks. Since March, Muhammad Ali's French-trained forces had routed the previously victorious Greeks in battle after battle. While the viceroy was on his way to becoming the most unpopular man in Europe, in Lyon the newspapers suddenly made his giraffe the most famous thing in France.

One newspaper reported:

> *Today the Giraffe toured a part of the city, accompanied by her keepers, a numerous picket of police, and a great crowd of the curious. The courteous animal did not fail to visit the Prefect, who accorded her the welcome due to a beautiful stranger. In order to protect her from the cold temperature, she was dressed in a mantle of waxed taffeta. The extraordinary temperature that has afflicted us for several days seems to redouble its rigor. Today the cold was so intense that snow fell on the heights near Lyon.*

Saint-Hilaire [Zarafa's owner] recorded that while they were in Lyon, the temperature fell below forty-three degrees Fahrenheit.

The newspapers ran daily reports and a long two-part essay on the giraffe by Saint-Hilaire, who also received praising reviews for his inspirational address to local students.

Lyon was interesting that week. Besides Zarafa and her exotic retinue—on view twice a day under the magnificent linden trees at the south side of the huge place Bellecour, "along the promenade of the flower sellers"—there was a grisly murder-suicide and an execution at which "all the convicts were present," a deterrent that caused the newspaper reporter to editorialize on the necessity of substituting "in our penal laws a system of correction for a system of vengeance."

Also that week at la place Bellecour, the papers advertised:

Messrs. Gulley and Smitt, of London, have the honor to offer to the public a superb collection of living serpents . . . every day from 11 in the morning to 8 in the evening, and composed of the following:

1. *The Rattlesnake, the only one to appear in France in the last 25 years;*
2. *The Serpent of Anaconda;*
3. *The Boa Constrictor;*
4. *The Embroidered Serpent;*
5. *The Harlequin Serpent.*

In addition, two Crocodiles of the Nile; the head of an Indian chief. . . . One is also able to see there a Giant, 6' 6" tall, aged 18 years. . . . The serpents are fed every Thursday at 3 P.M.

. . . After being received by the king, Zarafa was put on daily public exhibition at le Jardin du Roi. In the last three weeks of July 1827, 60,000 people came to see her. She was soon the subject of songs and instrumental music, poems and vaudeville skits, and anonymous political satires criticizing the king's censorship of the press. Unlike her short-lived companion in London, Zarafa became a tool but never the object of journalistic ridicule. Paris adored her.

Children playing in the parks of Paris bought snacks of gingerbread giraffes. Their mothers wore their hair *à la Girafe,* coiffured so high that they had to ride on the floors of their carriages. That summer the *Journal of Women and Fashion* reported the chic of "a necklace *à la Girafe,* a narrow ribbon from which is suspended a pink heart or better yet a small locket of the seraglio in the form of the amulet seen around the neck of the Giraffe at le Jardin du Roi."

The most stylish colors of that year's fashion season were "belly of Giraffe," "Giraffe in love," "Giraffe in exile." Men wore "Giraffic" hats and ties, and a magazine of the day diagrammed instructions for tying a gentleman's cravat *à la Girafe.*

Zarafamania was everywhere—in textiles and wallpaper, crockery and knickknacks, soap, furniture, topiary—anywhere her distinctive spots or long-necked shape could be employed. The recently invented claviharp was renamed the "piano-Giraffe." That winter's influenza was "Giraffe flu"; and people inquired of the sick, "How goes the Giraffe?"

from ZARAFA

The Survivor

PAUL D. BUCHANAN

Captain Frederick Benteen's small party from the Seventh Cavalry set out on the afternoon of June 27, 1876. The men on horseback rode nervously toward Little Bighorn River and the valley that surrounded it. As they crossed the summit of the little hill, calamity lay before them. Everywhere, as far as the eye could see, bodies of fallen United States Cavalry soldiers lay in pools of blood. More than 200 men, the entirety of four troops led by General George A. Custer, had been destroyed by the Sioux warriors of Crazy Horse and Sitting Bull.

Suddenly, a slight trace of movement could be detected off in the distance. As they approached, the soldiers found a large brown horse standing alone in a flat near the Indian village, like a sentinel at some military graveyard. Seven bullets had pierced the flesh of the steed: one through the neck, one just behind the front shoulder (passing through the lungs), and one through the hindquarters, with the rest apparently having nicked the flesh at various points. This was the mount of Captain Myles Keogh, a subordinate commander under General Custer. (It was later discovered that one of Keogh's legs had been broken by the same bullet that had penetrated behind the horse's front shoulder.) The mount's name was Comanche.

How the horse had managed to remain standing was beyond imagination.

Many theories have attempted to explain exactly what happened in southern Montana on June 25, 1876. Historians have pointed out that the battle would not have occurred had white men, greedy for gold and confident in the idea of "manifest destiny," not trespassed on the Sioux territory, and sought to push the natives off their land. This was just another example of the betrayal and deception played out by the Europeans, and the massacre of Custer and his men was the last desperate stand by the Sioux to protect their land and their culture.

Of the battle itself, some have said that Custer ignored warnings that 2000 to 4000 Sioux waited for his 250 soldiers. Others have said that had he brought just one Rodman gun or one Gatling gun with him, the battle's outcome would have been substantially reversed. Still others have accused Custer of seeking gold in the area himself, citing his personal avarice as the motivation for his foolish campaign. Whether due to greed, arrogance, incompetence, or—as some have suggested—derangement, one thing is for sure: The battle was a disaster for the Seventh Cavalry. And Comanche was the last living thing on the battlefield from Custer's side.

Badly wounded, the horse had not been captured by Sioux, as was the custom for healthy horses. Comanche was brought back to Fort Riley, Kansas, 63 miles west of Topeka, where the Seventh Cavalry was stationed. Through the winter of 1876–77, Comanche was nursed back to health by a Lieutenant Godfrey of the Seventh Cavalry, and by a blacksmith. Following the return of Comanche's health, Colonel Samuel D. Sturgis issued a special set of orders regarding the care and comfort of the animal, stating

His kind treatment and comfort should be a matter of
special pride and solicitude of the Seventh Cavalry, to
the end that his life be prolonged to the utmost limit.
Wounded and scarred as he is, his very existence speaks
in terms more eloquent than words of the desperate
struggle against overwhelming numbers; of the hope-
less conflict; and of the heroic manner in which all
went down on that fatal day. . . .

Among the details of Sturgis's orders were that Comanche
would be provided a special stall; would never be ridden under
any circumstance; would never be pressed into work of any
kind; and would be saddled, bridled, draped in mourning, and
led by a mounted trooper at all occasions of ceremony, in
memory of the soldiers who died tragically at Little Bighorn.
Comanche's life was transformed to one of utmost luxury—for
a horse, at least. He made several parade appearances, outfitted as Sturgis had ordered, and continued to live in his special stall.

On November 7, 1891, at the ripe age of 31, Comanche
died. The remains were presented to Professor Lewis Lindsay
Dyche of the University of Kansas, at the taxidermy laboratory.
Dr. Dyche set about preserving and mounting the remains, and
when he was done, the story goes, he sent a bill for $400 to the
Seventh Cavalry for his services. With the bill was a note, in-
forming the Cavalry that they could forego the invoice if they
would allow him to keep Comanche at the museum at the university. The Seventh Cavalry agreed, and Comanche has been
there ever since.

After all these years, Comanche remains a focal point of
interest for thousands of visitors to the Dyche Museum at the

University of Kansas. The viewers come to study the symbol of the struggle between native and immigrant people; the link in the transformation of wilderness to civilization; and the remains of the last living being at the Battle of Little Bighorn.

from FAMOUS ANIMALS OF THE STATES

Juneau's Official Greeter

ROBERTA SANDLER

$\mathcal{A}$ll those who travel to Juneau, Alaska, by water are welcomed at the dock by a dog named Patsy Ann. She doesn't bark. She doesn't wag her tail. She doesn't even respond when you call her.

That's because Patsy Ann is a bronze statue that sits imposingly and silently in the middle of Patsy Ann Square, which borders Juneau's Gastineau Channel.

The real Patsy Ann was a Staffordshire bull terrier who arrived in Juneau as a newborn pup in late 1929 with her human family. Her family didn't keep her once they realized she was deaf and could not bark.

The dog was taken in by a second family, but for unknown reasons was later abandoned by them as well. Patsy Ann then became an orphan who freely roamed the streets of Juneau.

Patsy Ann limited her daily wanderings to the downtown area, where local merchants and residents grinned at the sight of her happily loping from business to business.

Though Patsy Ann was an orphan, the Longshoremen's Hall became her nightly home. For her, it was the most logical place for warmth and sleep because she spent so much of her time on the docks. The deaf dog possessed a most remarkable ability. Whenever a ship neared Gastineau Channel, Patsy Ann was somehow able to "hear" its whistle, even if the ship was as much as a half-mile away. At once, the terrier would scamper down to the wharf to await the ship's arrival.

Juneau's residents had no idea how Patsy Ann was able to sense the imminent approach of a ship, anymore than they could figure out how the dog knew at exactly which dock she should wait. But they learned to trust her unerring judgment.

One afternoon, townspeople gathered at the appointed dock to await an incoming ship. Patsy Ann joined the expectant crowd and then suddenly ran to a different dock. Everyone was perplexed by her behavior until they realized they had been given misinformation. The ship entered the channel and berthed at the very dock where the terrier was waiting!

Patsy Ann may have loved the local people who fed her and fondly patted her. She may have felt cared for by the longshoremen. But Patsy Ann's primary happiness came from sitting on the docks as she waited to welcome the ships.

It was appropriate, then, in 1934, for Juneau's mayor to proclaim Patsy Ann "the official greeter of Juneau, Alaska."

That same year, the city passed an ordinance stating that all dogs must be licensed. After an animal-control worker impounded Patsy Ann and threatened to euthanize the stray, several of the locals chipped in to pay for her license and to buy a bright red collar for her. She was again free to continue her lookout duty.

For thirteen years, nearly all the days of her life, the wagging tail and the happy-go-lucky presence of the little dog brought a pleasant constancy to the lives of Juneau residents. She could not hear them say "good girl," but she saw their smiles and felt their affection.

Then, in 1942, Patsy Ann died of natural causes.

Members of the saddened community placed Patsy Ann's body in a small wooden casket and lowered it into Gastineau Channel. Now she would forever be tied to the hearts of Juneau's people and to the tranquil waters she loved to watch.

Nearly fifty years after Patsy Ann's death, a campaign was waged to memorialize the terrier. A small patch of land at the Gastineau wharfside was converted into what is now Patsy Ann Square, and a larger-than-life bronze statue was commissioned—complete with a bronze collar that rests at its base.

Today at the foot of the square, gaily-colored flowers bloom, and people sit on benches and gaze out at the horizon, just as the bronze Patsy Ann does.

Patsy Ann, adopted and loved by all the residents of Juneau, is still the official greeter for her city. The statue of the little dog who could not hear sits forever next to a wooden sign, her bronzed presence echoing the words printed there: Welcome to Juneau, Alaska.

Laika, Space Dog

BONNIE BERGEN

$\mathcal{T}$en short days in space opened the universe to earthbound mankind. Laika, a tiny 11-pound Russian spitz-type stray rescued from the streets of Moscow, with a supply of oxygen was launched into space on November 3, 1957 aboard Sputnik II in an orbit of historic proportions. The first living being to orbit the Earth, with no means of return, this brave female withstood what was undoubtedly a horrendous blast-off, disorienting sensations of weightlessness, and 10 days of utter isolation. Wired with sensors sending information to Earth, she provided critical information, paving the way for humankind to follow.

We can only guess at the feelings and thoughts of the Russian team who hurled her into the desolation of space, but someone there must have loved her. Someone there must have judged this pioneering effort warranted the loss of her life and mourned that reality. Would she have chosen this path, were she asked? My guess is yes. My sweet soft clinging golden retriever would have passed up such an invitation, but a bravehearted, independent, versatile little dog would probably have welcomed the adventure, leapt at the opportunity, and reveled in its uniqueness—at least at first.

The spitz-type dog, thought by some to be the first purebred dog group, has an impressive and highly versatile membership, including the fearless Japanese akita, the autocratic aloof Chinese chow, the sensible Dutch keeshond watchdog, the faithful Finnish spitz hunter, and the vivacious pomeranian, itself a descendant of Icelandic and Laplandic sled dogs. Laika's genetic credentials were undoubtedly well-researched before she received this honor. Chosen from among the many animals tested by Russian scientists, Laika was trained to eat a jelly-like food, wear the equivalent of a space suit, and handle simulated rocket engine noise and vibrations from inside an extremely small space capsule. The scientists' selection criteria—including a calm demeanor—was risky at best, since it could be proven successful only by the actual space flight. The training was also speculative. Yet they found what they were looking for in Laika, a little dog with a big soul willing to reach for the moon, stars, and beyond. A lesser dog might not have gone the distance, leaving man's future in space in doubt. But Laika did go the distance, earning her rightful place in history.

from ANIMAL FAIR

Pony Express

KATE PETTY

When the little mustang came into view, the crowd began to clap and cheer.

Her rider, Johnny Fry, led her into the packed town square of St. Joseph, Missouri, that warm April evening in 1860. Johnny checked the mail pouch on the mustang's back for the last time as she snorted excitedly.

A cannon boomed. They were away! The mustang raced off into the evening twilight, leaving the cheering crowds far behind.

Horse and rider had entered history as the first ever Pony Express team.

In 1860 there were no such things as telephones and fax machines. If you lived on the west coast of the United States, keeping up to date with the latest news on the east coast was almost impossible. It could take more than a month for mail to travel across the continent by wagon.

The Pony Express was a horse relay designed to keep the mail moving day and night. It cut down the time taken for mail to reach California to just eight days.

Each horse and rider galloped at top speed to the next station. The rider leaped off the exhausted horse shouting "Pony rider coming!" The mail was transferred to a fresh horse and the rider galloped off again on his new mount.

There were 157 relay stations, and riders changed horses about six to eight times.

The teams risked death together on a daily basis.

Much of the route lay through the homelands of Native Americans, some of whom declared war on the white invaders of their territory.

One of the bravest riders was "Pony Bob" Haslam. In May 1860 he arrived at a station in Nevada to find the keeper dead and all the horses gone. He set out for the next station, which was 40 miles (64 kilometers) away.

"I knew I had to carry on. As I rode through the night, I kept watching my pony's ears. I knew he'd hear any Indian ambush before I did."

At the next station he persuaded the keeper to leave with them. Bob and his tireless horse saved the man's life—the next night, that station was attacked.

The Pony Express teams rode across rocky mountain passes and wide, empty plains in scorching sun, pouring rain, and freezing blizzards. If their rider fell off, some brave horses carried on alone to the next station.

The final stop was Sacramento, California. Crowds of eager people would gather to watch the arrival of the last rider on the route bringing them their mail and newspapers.

The success of the Pony Express teams proved that it was possible for the east and west coast to keep in touch. It was a milestone on the way to modern America. The horses and riders that ran the Pony Express were real pioneers.

The Pony Express is remembered today by horse lovers

who ride the express's desert tracks for pleasure. Their journeys pay tribute to the riders of 1860, who insisted that "the
mail must get through."

from HORSE HEROES

GREAT PERFORMERS

"I still remember the thrill I felt when the Lone Ranger got on his horse and went after the bad guys. Silver was my hero."

ELLIOT ROBERTS

*N*ow we're talking about celebrities, the dogs, cats, dolphins, whales, elephants, horses and a few other animals who have given us countless hours of pleasure. We've seen them in circuses when we were kids, and in movies and television for as long as we can remember. They made us laugh and cry and we loved every minute of it.

But so did they. From what we know of these talented performers, most of them didn't come from happy homes. Many came from animal shelters where they were spotted by trainers with an eye for talent. All they needed was plenty of love and patience to bring out the best in them. And they certainly returned in kind.

Tracker

PEG KEHRET

$\mathcal{T}$racker began life as an unwanted puppy. Along with his eleven brothers and sisters, he was left at the Humane Society before he was old enough to be separated from his mother.

When this happens, the Humane Society places the puppies in foster homes with volunteers who will give them the extra care and attention (often including middle-of-the-night feedings) that such young animals need. The volunteers take the place of the mother dog.

Animals who go to foster homes as babies are often especially loving and gentle as adults. Because they receive lots of affection and tender care at an early age, they give great love in return. Pups who are left alone and not handled regularly do not learn to enjoy human companionship.

Tracker is a mixed-breed dog—probably part collie and perhaps part German shepherd or Akita. Perhaps. It's hard to tell for sure, and the people who brought the puppies in did not know or care. Tracker has a face like a collie's, with a long snout and expressive eyes. He has smooth white fur with a few large brown spots. A long, waving tail and one ear that flops over at the tip give him a distinctive look.

Whatever his breed, he got along well in foster care, and when he was old enough to be adopted, he was returned to the Humane Society. That's where he was at the age of eight weeks when Anne Gordon found him.

Anne is an animal trainer. With a college degree in biology and a minor in animal behavior, plus three years' experience as a zookeeper at Seattle's Woodland Park Zoo, Anne started her own company: Anne's Animal Actors. She trains wild and domestic animals of all kinds and prepares them to act in television shows, commercial productions, and movies. They also model for magazine and newspaper ads.

By the time she found Tracker, Anne was well known and highly sought after. Her credits included the movies *Homeward Bound, Free Willie 2, The Good Son, Home for the Holidays,* and the television series *Rescue 911.*

Anne did not need another dog, but when she saw Tracker she was so taken by his good looks and eager-to-please personality that she decided to give him a home.

Anne had adopted other dogs and cats from the Seattle/ King County Humane Society. She had also adopted animals from the Portland, Oregon, Humane Society and from the shelters of other animal welfare agencies. All became part of her business and members of her family.

Tracker went to Anne's home, deep in the woods in northern Washington State, where her other animal actors also live. Home for Anne Gordon and her four-legged friends is not merely a house. It is wooded acreage where each animal's needs are met.

Four wolves live in a half-acre of fenced forest. A pair of beavers, one male and one female, have side-by-side pens, each complete with its own swimming tub. When Anne bought these beavers from a fur farm, she saved their lives.

Two red foxes run to the fence to greet Anne whenever

they see her coming. A pair of mule deer, veteran actors with many credits, have an entire fenced acre of woods all to themselves. Two racoons, who were found orphaned as babies, amble about in their special enclosure.

The dog kennel contains a variety of mixed-breed dogs, each with its own spacious run and snug doghouse. When Anne walks to the kennel, every dog rushes to lick her hand. Each gets a turn to be out of the kennel every day, galloping around Anne's property. And they receive ongoing training to keep their acting skills sharp. Anne's assistants help care for and train the animals, and they take over for Anne when she is away.

At first Tracker lived inside Anne's house so she could bond with him and socialize him. The raccoons were babies then, and Tracker happily tolerated them as they climbed on his back and tried to play with his tail. This interaction was important because an animal actor must be able to get along with other animals of all kinds.

Anne began working with Tracker every day, teaching him all the basic obedience commands such as sit and stay. All of Anne's training is done with hand signals rather than voice commands so that she can direct her animals while they are being filmed.

When Tracker had mastered basic obedience, he began to accompany Anne when she took other animals on location. He watched while other dogs acted in films or got their pictures taken for magazines.

By going along at a young age, Tracker got used to the bright lights and noise and people. He learned to pay attention only to Anne's commands and not be distracted by anything else that was going on around him.

Tracker proved to be a quick learner who loved to go to work with Anne. Soon he auditioned for his own first part and got it.

Tracker's first acting job was in a television commercial for the Oregon State Lottery. Anne drove him to Portland, where the commercial was filmed. Tracker's part was not difficult; he had to lie on the floor with his head down, next to a woman in a chair. Then, when Anne gave the signal, Tracker was supposed to lift his head and perk up his ears as if something exciting had happened.

Tracker performed flawlessly. Anne knew he was a fine actor. She continued to teach him new commands and included agility training in his lessons.

In agility training, Tracker learned to go through tunnels, climb ladders, walk on elevated walks, and do a variety of jumps. Agility training is good for film work because it gives a dog confidence. Tracker seemed to like practicing these new skills.

A few months after Tracker made the lottery commercial, a movie producer contacted Anne. His company, The Edge Productions, planned to make a feature film based on the book *Summer of the Monkeys* by Wilson Rawles. There was a major role for a dog.

Whenever Anne is asked to provide animal actors, she first figures out exactly what the animal will be required to do. She reads the script and has the director fax her storyboards that spell out specific behavior for each scene. She also talks to the director by phone, to be certain there is no misunderstanding.

After Anne read *Summer of the Monkeys,* she knew that several of her dogs had the skills to play the part of the hound dog in the movie. Although the dog's role was important, it did not require doing any unusual or sophisticated tricks.

She sent the movie's director photos of the dogs who she felt could handle the role. She included Tracker. After seeing the photos, the director wanted to watch the dogs in action, so Anne made a video and sent that.

The director liked Tracker's unusual looks and the natural way he acted on screen. The decision was made: Tracker had his first part in a movie! He was two years old.

Four chimpanzees were also scheduled to work in this movie, so the first step was to make sure Tracker would get along with them. Although he was used to a wide variety of animals at Anne's house, he had never seen a chimpanzee.

Tracker and Anne flew to Sacramento, California, where the chimps lived. While Anne sat with Tracker, the owner of the chimps carried the youngest one, a two-year-old, into the room. He sat holding the little chimp while Anne stayed with Tracker. The chimp and the dog looked at each other. Tracker's tail wagged. The chimp leaned toward him. Clearly, the animals were curious, and each wanted to go closer to the other.

The two owners cautiously allowed the animals to approach each other. Soon the baby chimp was hanging on Tracker's tail and then sitting on his back. Tracker appeared to enjoy the fun as much as the chimp did.

One by one, the older chimps were also introduced. Tracker got along fine with all of them. He and Anne flew back home, where Anne spent the next six weeks preparing Tracker to do his role.

Because Tracker's role required a lot of running, Anne needed a second dog to act as his double. This was in case they had to shoot some of the running scenes over and over. She did not want Tracker to get too tired, and she had no way to control how many times the scenes would need to be repeated.

It was not easy to find another dog who looked even remotely like Tracker. With his thoroughly mixed heritage, he has a one-of-a-kind appearance, which is what attracted the movie's director in the first place.

After a lengthy search, Anne finally borrowed a dog named Scooter from a friend. Scooter had been adopted from the Oregon Humane Society in Portland where Anne's friend worked.

Scooter closely matched Tracker in size and shape, and the coloring on her face was similar. Best of all, she had received both obedience and agility training. With natural vegetable dyes, Scooter's fur was darkened in places to make her look more like Tracker.

Anne, the two dogs, and an assistant trainer drove from Seattle to Saskatoon, Saskatchewan, in Canada, where the movie was to be filmed. They settled into a lakeside cabin that had been rented for them. The next day they drove past wheat and canola fields to the studio.

Tracker met Corey Sevier, the boy who would play the lead role in *Summer of the Monkeys.* Corey also had acted in the television series *Lassie,* so he was experienced at working with a dog.

Six chimps were on location to play the four chimps in the film. Just as Tracker needed a double to be sure he did not get overtired, the chimps had extra help, too. Anne and the owner of the chimps did not want to harm their animal friends. The American Humane Association also watches out for the welfare of all animal actors while they are at work on a movie or TV set.

For an animal, the hardest part of acting is to concentrate

only on the trainer. This is especially difficult when more than one animal is in a project.

Tracker had several scenes with the chimps. He had to watch Anne and obey her signals without getting distracted by the chimps. They were nearby with *their* trainer, who was also giving them hand signals.

After six weeks of rehearsal, the filming began. All went smoothly until the scene which required a chimp to run out of the woods toward the camera. A few seconds later, Tracker was to chase the chimp. The chimp was supposed to look scared of the dog and run away as fast as he could.

The cameras rolled. The chimp was released. The chimp's trainer stood behind the camera, giving the hand signal to the chimp for him to come. The chimp obeyed and ran toward the camera—until Tracker was released behind him.

As soon as the chimp heard Tracker running after him, he stopped and waited for his friend. Dog and chimp then tore around in circles, playing happily with each other!

It took several retakes before the scene captured on film looked as if the chimp, terrified, was running from the dog.

Twice, the filming of scenes where Tracker had to run for a long distance had to be repeated so many times that Anne called for Scooter to take Tracker's place while Tracker rested.

When the filming ended, Scooter went home to Portland, and Tracker and Anne returned to their woodland home. Tracker seemed glad to see all the other animals again. He got a well-earned rest while he waited for the next call for an animal actor with his special looks and skills.

Tracker began life unwanted and unloved, as do far too many puppies. Every animal shelter staff member has heard the words, "I can't find homes for them all" hundreds of times.

Luckily for Tracker, he was taken to the Humane Society, where volunteer foster parents open their homes and hearts to puppies who are too young to be adopted. Because Tracker's foster parents held him, petted him, and kept him warm and fed, he developed into a happy, sociable puppy who liked people and was trainable.

Now Tracker is a movie star with a loving trainer, unusual animal friends, and a long career ahead of him.

from SHELTER DOGS

A Cat on Tour

PETER GETHERS

(Editor's Note: Norton, the author's cat, accompanied Peter Gethers on a national book tour. After all, the book was about Norton.)

The Four Seasons is where I always stay in L.A. It's convenient, classy, and perfect for conducting business. The staff is also extraordinarily nice to Norton. In fact, every Four Seasons is particularly gracious toward pets. In the Boston Four Seasons, they even have a pet room-service menu. I know this because when we stayed there, I was happy to find a large bowl filled with nuts when I walked into the room. Only I soon realized they weren't nuts but dog biscuits—and fairly tasty dog biscuits, I might add. Under the bowl was a small, printed sheet which was titled "Doggie Delights." The rest of the menu read as follows:

BARK, BARK!
(Main Courses)
#1 Ruff, Ruff, rrr . . .
(Quickly Broiled Beef Filet with natural broth $6.00)

#2   Aowh, Aohw, Aohwooooooo!
(Boneless "Safe to Eat" Lamb Chops $7.00)

#3   Woof! Woof! Grrr!
(Roasted Chicken Breast with natural gravy $5.50)

BARK!!!
(Side Dishes)

#1   Awwrr, Yip, Yip!
(Brown Rice $1.75)

#2   Grrrrrr . . .
(White Rice $1.75)

ARP! ARP!

(Assorted Ice Creams $2.00)

Needless to say, I called down to check this out. At first I thought it was a joke, but when the room-service person indignantly assured me it wasn't, I wanted to know why the menu was geared only for canine guests. The voice at the other end of the phone hemmed and hawed over that one but finally said he was sure that cats would also find the food quite delicious; the hotel was happy to admit that dogs were not the only four-legged connoisseurs.

It turned out the room-service maven was correct. Twenty minutes after I hung up, a waiter arrived. On the cart he wheeled in was an array of fine china. And on the china was a delicious—judging from Norton's considered reaction—chicken breast.

But even with the usual fine Four Seasons treatment, I still wasn't prepared for the greeting we got upon our arrival in L.A.

First of all, as the cab from the airport dropped me off in front of the hotel, I heard two men in black suits say, in muffled tones, "He's here." Surprised, I put the cat in his shoulder bag and we headed into the lobby. As we stepped inside, two more men in black suits said, "He's here. Get ready."

I knew Norton was popular, I thought to myself, but I felt a surprise party was just a tad excessive.

The entire lobby seemed abuzz as we walked toward the desk. There was a flurry of activity, people rushed toward me—reporters, hotel staff, more guys in black suits. I smiled broadly and Norton stuck his head out of the bag, craning his neck in his best E.T. impersonation—who are we to reject V.I.P. treatment?—and then we watched as everyone rushed toward us . . . and right past us. As even more guys in black suits stampeded by, saying things under their breath like, "Moving toward the elevator. Cover the doors," Norton and I casually glanced behind us—where the President of the United States was standing. Yup. George Bush was there for some kind of money-raising, glad-handing function. I suppose, if I'd really thought it through, I would have realized that Norton didn't need *all* of those Secret Service guys. Nonetheless, I confess to being just a tad disappointed.

Not for long, however.

With Bush out of the way, I found that cat and I were the only guests remaining in the lobby. So when I heard a woman's voice say, "Wait a second, I think he's here," I again turned behind me to see which top-notch celebrity had breezed in. Mel Gibson? Liz Taylor? The cast from "Beverly Hills 90210"? I was determined not to be sucker-punched again.

So I was even more confused when I realized there was

nobody behind us, not even Herve Villachaize. Norton and I were *it* as far as lobby loiterers.

Another woman, this time from behind the check-in desk, said, quite clearly, "It *is* him. He's here!"

This led to a couple of exclamatory bursts from other women, all exceedingly attractive—one at the cashier's desk, one from behind the concierge's counter—along the lines of, "We've been waiting for you! We're *so* glad you're here!"

I decided that this was definitely more like it. Until, naturally, I was forced to accept the fact that once again I was not their obscure object of desire. The real target was not nearly so obscure.

"Norton," the woman at the front desk cooed with her arms held out in welcome, "we are *so* glad to see you!"

Now, I've stayed at the Four Seasons ten or fifteen times. When I'm there by myself, they're certainly friendly—but no one ever holds her arms out to me and scratches me under the chin while shrieking how cute I look. Norton had stayed there four or five times—and no one had really even done that to *him* before. At least, not quite in this fashion. Because that night, as we checked in, just about every person who worked on the ground floor came out to fuss over their smallest, grayest guest. It turned out that the publicist for the book had sent a few copies over to the hotel several days before. They'd been passed around and read and Norton was now clearly on the Four Seasons' "A" list of desirable celebrities.

"We've upgraded you to a Four Seasons suite," the desk clerk said, smiling at the cat.

"We think you'll like it," another said, petting him.

"And we've got a few surprises for you up there," another one told him, scratching his stomach (by this time, he was lying on his back on top of the check-in counter; I was a little startled at how easily he'd succumbed to life in the L.A. fast lane).

I was starting to wonder if they were going to take Norton's credit card, since it was pretty obvious I was an afterthought, but no such luck. For that part they deigned to talk to me.

When we were finally shown to our room, we had indeed been upgraded to a suite. Norton also had a litter box already set up in the bathroom. On the floor by the TV were two elegant dishes, one for water—with a bottle of Evian next to it!—and one to fill with the cans of food that were stacked on top of the end table. And on the desk in the living room was a gift-wrapped box with a note taped to it.

Flattered and pleased, I tore open the package—only to find that it was a can of shrimp-flavored Pounce. Deflated—I don't know what I'd expected; I think I had my heart set on a lovely crystal goblet—I also opened the note, which was from the manager of the hotel. It read (handwritten):

> *Dear Norton,*
>
> *Welcome back to the Four Seasons! My cats, Nicholas and Alexandra, would love to meet you someday . . . you sound like a really neat guy.*
>
> *Enjoy your stay.*
>
> > *Kathleen Horrigan*
> > *Hotel Manager*

I prowled around the room (both rooms!), hoping that perhaps Kathy Horrigan had also left a small basket of fruit lying around for me, but not a chance. It was clear from the

very beginning that Norton was the star of this little sojourn.
And from his contented meowing—over by his bottle of Evian
water—I could tell he was not unhappy about it.

The highlight of our travels around the country came at the
very beginning of the trip in L.A. when the publisher threw a
party to celebrate publication of the book. It wasn't just a regular humdrum party with potato chips and clam dip. For Norton,
they threw a bash at Spago, the most famous restaurant in the
country, run by Wolfgang Puck, arguably the most celebrated
chef in the world.

Not that I'm jaded or anything, but I'd been to Spago plenty
of times. In fact, my mother works with Wolf (she helped
him write his last cookbook) and she's part of the unofficial
Spago family.

Norton had never dined there, however. In fact, no cat had
ever dined at Spago before—until Norton broke the barrier
that night. Broke it in style, I might add.

They closed the restaurant for a few hours for our private
party. The guest of honor—a hint: not me—was given his own
table, upon which he sat in a princelike fashion and let all the
guests come over and pay homage. Wolf, whose renowned
specialties are pizzas covered with such delicacies as smoked
salmon, wild mushrooms, or caviar, made Norton a pizza covered with Norton's favorite delicacy—Pounce. The pastry chef,
an amazing woman named Mary (who, in honor of an annual
trip I make to Las Vegas with a bunch of friends, once made a
cake in the shape of Sammy Davis, Jr.), baked small cakes and
cookies with cat paws and cat whiskers all over them. I was
congratulated once or twice by the fifty or so guests, but mostly
they fussed over Norton. Many of them had never been out in

public with him and they couldn't believe how human he acted (they thought that was a compliment; we know better). During the several hours we were there, Norton perched himself on his table/throne, ate when he felt like it, drank a little milk when he was in the mood, allowed journalists to take his picture, let children talk to him as if he were a grown-up (and I mean a grown-up person, not a grown-up cat), and permitted all his admirers to pet him, stroke him, and compliment him. He even let the manager of the restaurant repeatedly refer to him as "Norman" without swatting at his ankle.

The highlight of the evening, however, was Wolf's wife, Barbara Lazaroff, the designer of and guiding force behind Spago and all of Wolf's other restaurants. Barbara, who's extremely attractive and even more flamboyant, strode into the party wearing a cat outfit. We're talking cat slippers—with whiskers and everything—cat pants, a cat sweater, and a cat hat. Norton, for one brief, shining moment, thought he'd met the ultimate member of the opposite sex, but eventually, to his disappointment, I'm sure, he realized that Barbara was just another admiring, if stunning, human.

After the Spago party, the rest of our tour was fairly typical—considering that one of the authors on tour was a four-legged feline. Following L.A., for the hardcover and the paperback versions of the first book about our adventures together, Norton and I went to San Diego, San Francisco, Portland, Seattle, Miami, Dayton, Rochester, Detroit, Dallas, and Philadelphia. (After the West Coast tour, I told the publisher that a city a day was just too tough on my little pal. He was an extraordinary trouper and shockingly well behaved—just ask any of the couple of thousand people who came by to meet him—but, still, I felt it wasn't fair to cart him around all day, then put him on an airplane.

So, for the other cities, we were put on what I heard referred to as the "old author's tour." That meant we got an extra day or two in each city to ease the travel burden. Me, Norton, and James Michener.)

from A CAT ABROAD

Hollywood Hero

KATE PETTY

In 1932 a star was born. He was a beautiful golden color with a white, flowing mane and tail. Son of a palomino mare and a racehorse, Golden Cloud was to become the most famous horse of his day.

Golden Cloud made his big screen debut in 1938. His owners, Hudkin Stables, lent him out to play a part in the Hollywood film *The Adventures of Robin Hood.*

Later that year, Republic Studios decided to make a series of Westerns featuring the singing cowboy actor, Roy Rogers. They brought several horses round for Roy to audition. He fell for Golden Cloud the moment he climbed on to the horse's back.

While they were making their first film, *Under Western Stars,* Golden Cloud was renamed "Trigger" because he was so quick.

Roy loved Trigger so much that after their third film, he bought Trigger for $2,500. From then on, they became full-time partners.

Trigger loved the camera. He often stole the show from Roy Rogers with a well-timed yawn or a graceful dance step.

He knew over 60 tricks. He could walk 150 steps on his hind legs, stamp his hoof to count, and draw a gun from a holster.

Trigger became one of the most popular characters in

show business. He starred in 87 films and 101 TV shows, and once even had a party in the Grand Ballroom of the Astor Hotel in New York City.

Like a true star, Trigger made special personal appearances. He always traveled in style, carried his own horse-sized passport, and signed his name with an X in hotel registers.

Trigger finally retired in 1957, and died in 1965, aged 33. Roy Rogers was heartbroken. He said he had lost "the greatest horse who ever came along."

from HORSE HEROES

Rin Tin Tin

RAYMOND LEE

On the morning of September 15, 1918, Corporal Lee Duncan, with a small party of enlisted men headed by Captain George Bryant, left Toul in Lorraine, France, to look for a new field site for the 136th Aero Squadron.

Near noon they stumbled on an abandoned German war dog station that had been heavily shelled. In a blasted dugout Duncan discovered a half-starved mother dog and five puppies. The Captain and the Corporal knew they couldn't stop the war for the cold- and shock-shivering little family and yet . . . The Corporal suggested taking them back to the hangar; the Captain nodded his approval. On the detail's return from the tour, after struggling with the mother who thought they were going to kill her babies, they rescued the litter.

That tattered second on the battle-torn wastes of No-Man's-Land was going to prove to be one of destiny for many people.

Many times asked why he suggested saving the little family, Lee said, "It was my mother, I am sure. Like I heard her voice even out there. When I was a kid she always reminded me to be kind to animals. She said, 'A boy who loves animals can love people twice as much.'"

At the war's end Duncan brought back two of the puppies while Captain Bryant took the mother and remaining three.

Duncan named them Nannette and Rin Tin Tin after the finger-length dolls the French soldiers and airmen always carried with them for good luck.

Disembarking in New York, Duncan had to leave Nannette behind because she had contracted pneumonia. In Chicago he received a wire she had died. Considering her smarter than Rin Tin Tin he was deeply shaken by her passing. As the troop train continued on to California Rinty snuggled up to his master and licked his face. It was a million dollar kiss he never forgot.

Out of that mud-hole Lee Duncan had snatched a movie star that would one day earn more than a million dollars. Known as "the mortgage-lifter," because of his fantastic drawing power at the box-office, Rin Tin Tin was the property of Warner Brothers Studios in the lean days and, before and after sound, the star who held off the creditors. Insured for $100,000 he had his own production unit and several hundred men and women made a good living working for a dog.

In such Twenties' hits as *The Night Cry, Clash of Wolves, A Dog of the Regiment* and *The Man Hunter,* Rin Tin Tin ran the gamut of emotions as capably as any human star of the period.

And he lived like one as Joel Sayre commented:

"Rin had his own valet and chef, and his private limousine and chauffeur. The Warner's technical staff was as eager in his service. Every Rin Tin Tin epic was climaxed by his arrival to the rescue in the nick of time, so that he was frequently called upon to leap full speed through closed windows. To safeguard Duncan's priceless property from having his beauty marred or his jugular severed by glass fragments, windowpanes of trans-lucent candy were contrived, and Rin sailed through them with breath-stopping effect. As a reward Duncan would sometimes let him eat fragments of the candy pane.

"Another wonderful stunt of Rin's was getting past a locked door by scrambling over its transom. Rin of course, could jump higher than any transom, but getting through one in a hurry was always something of a tight fit for a ninety-pound dog. To make things easier for him, cleats painted to match the wood—thereby rendered invisible on the film—enabled Rin to run straight up doors with the speed of a cat. Using the cleats he could enter a second-story window or even go up a twenty-foot wall at top speed and get on a roof. When he had a scene involving running through fire, special chemicals were used to prevent his being burned. There were other technical marvels, too, to assist him in his breath-taking feats."

As with most movie stars the love-light shone in Rinty's eyes. The beautiful girl's name was Nannette and their marriage was a social highlight in the Beverly Hills home Lee bought for them and himself. As motherhood followed and Nannette presented Rinty with a batch of little ones a skilled nursemaid was hired.

Rinty had four sons who stood on their own feet as dog stars and Rinty IV became a sleeper-success on TV in a popular series.

Regarding Rin Tin Tin's amazing antics before the camera, Lee Duncan had this to say:

"Everyone has always wanted to know the secret of Rinty's training. He has never been trained. He's just an educated dog.

"A trained or broken dog wears a look of fear while he is performing his set tricks. He is afraid of the whip if he fails to do them correctly. Rin Tin Tin has never felt a whip. We simply understand each other and until you understand your dog you can never hope to teach him anything.

"The surest way of learning to understand your dog is to spend as much time as you can with him. Don't pet him every minute, but always reward him with a loving pet when he has done something well.

"Sometimes other boys will tell you, 'Your dog is a coward. See him jump,' and they burst an inflated paper bag in the dog's face.

"Now that's no way to begin. There is no excuse for frightening him ever. If you want to teach him not to be afraid of the popping noise, try bursting the bag at a distance. Then come a little closer each time until he has gradually become accustomed to the sound and he will not be shocked.

"Dogs, like children, can't stand temptation, so when you go away and leave your dog in the house, don't leave your bedroom slippers on the floor for him to play with. If they are there, he will want to play with them and after a while he will play and chew too hard and when you come home there won't be any slippers.

"If you are careless enough to let this happen, don't scold your dog afterward, because he won't know what you are scolding him for. The time for scolding is when he is in the act of destroying the slippers. Then you may take him and say, 'Shame' or 'no,' and soon he will learn that the slippers are to be let alone.

"You will be able to teach your own dog many things as you begin to understand his ways and not until then.

"As to Rinty, I just understand him, sometimes I think he understands me more and that is why there isn't anything the director asks him to do he can't do. He knows he's a movie star and therefore must do his duty as such."

What was the extraordinary relationship between this man and his dog? Was it as simple as he has stated?

Rinty was a one-man dog. Only Lee Duncan could control

him. After the scene had been taken he would be a different animal entirely. He might bite the very actor he had just played an affectionate and touching moment with.

Charles Hargan, who played fight scenes with Rinty, told Duncan one day that if the dog bit him he'd bite him back. Duncan laughed and then stunt man and dog did the scene. Following the rough and tumble Rinty suddenly bit Hargan on one of his padded legs. Much to everyone's surprise, including the canine celeb, Hargan grabbed Rinty and bit him on the ear. Duncan quickly rushed to the rescue of his walking gold mine. But Rinty learned a lesson. He never nipped Hargan again and Hargan continued as his adversary.

D. Ross Lederman, who directed some of Rin Tin Tin's outstanding films, described the fascinating union between Duncan and Rinty:

"With Lee handling him, there was nothing a human actor could do that we couldn't get out of the dog. Lee would tell him and we'd get it, often the very first time.

"He was always on time, never made temperamental difficulties and almost never blew a scene. There was a lot of black on his head and back, and we always had trouble lighting him properly in those days. But I've seen him hold a pose for the electricians for thirty minutes without moving a whisker.

"It was amazing how he'd understand what Lee said to him. If there was a scene with four or five separate moves or actions in it, Lee would draw chalk marks on the floor—as we sometimes used to do for the human actors—and the dog would follow them perfectly. Lee never struck the dog nor lost his temper, and the dog had ears and eyes only for him. They always worked together entirely by love.

"Rin Tin Tin *was* Lee Duncan . . . "

As dramatically as Rin Tin Tin was born into this turbulent world he left it in his fourteenth year.

On August 10, 1932, after a playful twilight romp on their front lawn, Rinty jumped into Duncan's arms. He was dead weight. As Duncan fell to his knees he attracted the attention of his neighbor, Jean Harlow, who ran across the street.

As both cradled the beloved German Shepherd—born in war and ranging through depression and then reaching the summit of world popularity, acclaim and affection—his spirit passed like the shadows before the oncoming night. The screen's reigning love symbol Jean Harlow sobbed her heart out while Lee Duncan wept for a part of himself that also had died.

from NOT SO DUMB

Jumbo

PAUL D. BUCHANAN

The most famous animal of Connecticut is quite likely the most famous elephant in history, probably the most famous circus animal in history, perhaps even the most famous animal of all. Everything about Jumbo was jumbo, and his impact on Connecticut, the Eastern Seaboard, England, the English language, the American Public, and entertainment in general was equally colossal.

Jumbo was a male African elephant who stood more than 11 feet tall and weighed in excess of 13,000 pounds. He ate more than 300 pounds of food a day, washing it down with five buckets of water. The very word "jumbo" has been assimilated into the American parlance to mean anything gigantic or, according to Webster, "a very large specimen of its kind." Even today, beer, soft drink, pretzels, and peanuts, all come in "jumbo" size. This association with extravagance is a fitting tribute to an animal who was once the primary attraction of premier American showman and propagandist Phineus T. Barnum.

Jumbo was captured as a baby by Hamran Arabs in 1865. The Arabs sold him to a Bavarian named Johann Schmidt who, in turn, sold it to the Jardin des Plantes in Paris. At the time, the elephant who was to become Jumbo stood only four feet tall.

Disappointed, the director of the Jardin traded the baby elephant to the London Zoological Gardens for a rhinoceros.

In 1882, when the London Zoological Gardens sold Jumbo to P. T. Barnum for $10,000, a wave of melancholy swept through England. Jumbo had become a great favorite in that country. Britain's children, who had spent 17 years riding on the beast's back, wept openly in the streets. The English Parliament, and even Queen Victoria herself, joined in the plea for the London Zoo to renege on the contract, but to no avail. Jumbo the Elephant crossed the Atlantic Ocean aboard the *Assyrian Monarch,* arriving in New York on Easter Sunday.

The United States was more than ready to welcome an attraction such as Jumbo, as well as any other phenomenon Barnum was willing to present—or to exploit, as some would say. The country was enjoying the fruits of a post-war industrial revolution, and leisure activities such as baseball, harness racing, and circuses were finding their ways to the masses. America was also developing a new fascination with animal life, spawned by vigorous interest in the writings of Charles Darwin. Jumbo could not have arrived at a more advantageous time—especially for P. T. Barnum.

Jumbo was presented to the American public with the usual Barnum flare. One advertisement proclaimed, "His trunk is the size of an adult crocodile, his tail is as big as a cow's leg, and he made footprints in the sands of time resembling an indentation as if a very fat man had fallen off a very tall building." Thousands of children rode Jumbo's back, and Jumbo products—ranging from hats to cigars—sold by the score.

For the three years Jumbo lived in the United States, his winter quarters were at Waldemere, P. T. Barnum's fabulous estate at Bridgeport, Connecticut. While residing in Bridgeport,

Jumbo provided the services of a beast of burden for the Barnum estate.

It all came to a tragic end in September of 1885. At 9:00 on September 15, the circus was being loaded for departure from a performance at St. Thomas, Ontario, Canada. An attendant was leading Jumbo to his private car with his fellow performer, Tom Thumb (a baby elephant used to emphasize Jumbo's great girth). Suddenly an unscheduled freight train roared around the corner, headed straight for the elephants. The impact hurled Tom Thumb aside, and Jumbo incurred the brunt of the crash. The collision crushed Jumbo's massive skull, while smashing and derailing the engine and two cars. Jumbo rolled over to one side, and in a few moments, he died.

Barnum was never to find an attraction to replace Jumbo the Elephant. Barnum once estimated Jumbo had been seen by nine million Americans, easily the greatest single feature of Barnum's many great shows. Although the showman tried to minimize the loss, it was clear that the Barnum and Bailey Circus would never fully recover. As it turned out, neither would Barnum. He went into semi-retirement at Waldemere soon afterward, and died in 1891.

from FAMOUS ANIMALS OF THE STATES

Ballet on Horseback

KATE PETTY

"He's a lively one," said the stable lad, pointing toward the dark colt leading the race across the field.

The colt's name was Favory. He was one of the Lipizzaner foals born in the early 1980s at the Piber stud farm, where horses are bred for the Spanish Riding School.

"Look how much energy he's got," said the stable lad.

"Maybe too much," said one of the grooms. Favory was popular with the workers at the stud farm, but could he make it at the school? The groom knew that if Favory was going to perform at the school's regular displays, he had to have personality, discipline, and strength.

When Favory was three and a half years old his training began.

He traveled with the other new students to Vienna. Here in the school's Winter Riding Hall, horses train and perform dressage, a set of complicated steps that have been the same for centuries. The school is famous worldwide for how skillfully its horses can do dressage.

Hardest of all the steps are the "Airs above the ground," a series of amazing jumps that only the strongest horses can perform.

All the riders at the school were eager to see if any of the new students were strong and steady enough to make the grade.

Unfortunately, Favory didn't give a good first impression. He broke away from his groom and galloped around the hall, showing off. "We've got our work cut out with that one," said one of the riders.

Watching Favory closely was the First Chief Rider, the most experienced rider in the school. He liked horses with spirit. But did Favory have the self-control that he would need to perform the Airs?

There was only one way to find out.

The First Chief Rider decided to train Favory himself. He wanted to get the best out of Favory without changing his unique character.

For the first two weeks, the First Chief Rider led Favory gently by hand. Then he put a saddle on Favory and trained him on a rope called a lunge.

Favory hated the saddle, so the First Chief Rider only put it on for a few minutes at a time. Soon Favory let the First Chief Rider get on the saddle and ride him.

Then the First Chief Rider taught Favory how to focus his energy into performing dressage steps.

In just a few years, Favory was good enough to perform in the dressage section of the school's shows.

The school's sell-out shows are famous all over the world. The horses and riders perform dressage, the Airs, and a ballet to music.

The First Chief Rider was pleased with Favory's progress in the shows. Now it was time for the hardest task of all—to teach Favory the Airs.

The first Air that Favory learned was the *Levade*. He had to rear up and balance on his hind legs.

Strongly built horses go on to learn the *Courbette.* But Favory's lively personality made him ideally suited to the *Capriole.*

To perform this spectacular Air, Favory had to leap up with all four feet off the ground. Then, at the highest point of the jump he had to kick his back legs out behind him.

Favory practiced the Airs until he could do them perfectly every time. It was not long before the First Chief Rider gave him a wonderful reward.

As the show draws to a close, the First Chief Rider presents a fully trained stallion to demonstrate the *Capriole.* It must be a stallion with great talent and a calm mind.

"Let's go," said the First Chief Rider one evening to the stallion that he had chosen.

The audience gasped as a magnificent white horse trotted gracefully to the center of the arena.

It was Favory. At last he had the chance to show off his skills. He performed the Airs to perfection and the audience loved him. Favory was a star.

from HORSE HEROES

Scruffy in the Spotlight

VIRGINIA PHELPS CLEMENS

"Lights, action, roll 'em."

The shaggy little dog lay quietly on the braided rug in front of the television. Curled up in a ball, he rested his nose on his hind feet and the tip of his brown-and-white tail.

Suddenly, Scruffy lifted his head, pricked up his ears and looked toward the doorway. Some strange noises were coming from the front hall. Before he could get up to see what was going on, a miniature mule team pulling a tiny red-and-white-checkered chuck wagon charged around the corner.

The little dog sat right up with as surprised a look on his face as any human actor could make. He watched for a moment as the team and wagon darted under the edge of the living room rug. Finally, he couldn't stand it any longer.

Barking excitedly, Scruffy gave chase. The mules popped out from under the other side of the rug and galloped into the dining room. The dog dashed after them. Under the table and between the chairs the mules, swaying wagon, and dog went, twisting and turning around the legs of the furniture.

The driver of the wagon cracked his long, black whip and shouted encouragement to his team.

"Hi yup there, mules, get along."

The chase roared into the kitchen. The wagon's wheels rumbled across the floor as the little dog appeared to be catching up. One more step and Scruffy would be able to grab them. Suddenly, the mules leaped right through the closed door of a kitchen cabinet and disappeared, pulling the chuck wagon in after them.

The little dog skidded to a stop and stood in front of the cabinet with his head cocked and a puzzled look on his face. After waiting for a few seconds to see if the mules and wagon would reappear, he began barking angrily.

The dog's owner walked into the kitchen and over to the cabinet, where he took out a box of Chuck Wagon dog food. Tail wagging happily, Scruffy quickly sat up on his hind legs and waved his front paws in the air, begging for his dinner.

"Cut!"

. . . Scruffy was found by animal trainer Carl Miller in the Sherman Way Animal Shelter in North Hollywood, California. Mr. Miller felt sorry for him, so he paid $7.50 and took him home. Scruffy is a happy-go-lucky dog, described by Mr. Miller as "an accident looking for something to happen." He was full of mischief when first brought home. He ran away when being brushed, dug holes in the yard, and pulled clothes off the clothesline.

Scruffy was also naturally "toy crazy," which helped in training him. His reward for doing a trick correctly was to be able to play with a squeak toy.

In *The Ghost and Mrs. Muir,* Scruffy was supposed to walk alongside a boy on a beach. Scruffy didn't know the boy and wouldn't have walked with him, so they put his little squeak mouse in the boy's pocket. The boy would press his arm against the toy to make it squeak as he walked. Scruffy stayed right at his side, ears cocked and eyes on the boy's pocket.

from SUPER ANIMALS AND THEIR UNUSUAL CAREERS

Tom, Tony and Duke

RAYMOND LEE

$\mathcal{I}$n 1917 directors Sidney and Chester Franklin formed the Fox Kiddie Company of juveniles ranging from seven to ten years and playing grown-up parts in such classics as *Jack and the Beanstalk, Aladdin and His Lamp* and *Treasure Island.*

But my greatest thrill, and disappointment, came the day we began work on *Six Shooter Andy* starring the biggest three on the western panorama—Tom Mix, Tony, the wonder horse, and Duke, the Great Dane, with the Franklins directing.

My uncle, Hank Potts, a pioneer stunt and trick horseman was also on the picture and during a lull in the action he asked me how things were going.

"Well, this being our first day, us Fox Kiddies expected something really terrific to happen."

"Like what?"

"Like something the most terrific cowboy in the world would do."

"So?"

"So Tom rides on the set in a big shiny car with Tony behind in a trailer and Duke sitting in the front seat."

"Now, Ray, don't let that take any of the kick out of you. Tom drives his cars like his nags. Tom's all and more than's ever been said or written about him. Did you know he was once a Texas Ranger?"

"A Texas Ranger?"

"Right. And he was also a Rough Rider under Teddy Roosevelt and a volunteer in the Philippine uprisings. He also saw military service in the Orient during the Boxer Rebellion and was a Range Rider in El Paso."

"Wait 'til I tell the other kids!"

My uncle handed me a piece of chewing gum and popped one in his mouth himself and we both started chewing hard as he really shook me up with a story that had never been told.

"You wanna hear a horse story to end all horse stories?"

I nodded because I couldn't wag my tongue.

"It's hard to believe, but I once bought and sold a million dollar property and lost fifty cents on the deal."

Uncle Hank popped his gum and I tried but failed. I never could pop gum.

"Pat Crissman—Tom's manager—and me have been good friends since I first rode into pictures as a punk kid. Always looking around for a bargain in horse-flesh, we wandered down to Fifth and Central in L.A. to an auction. There weren't any bargains but not wanting to come back empty-handed we bought a sorrel pony for $12.50. Pat had only six bucks so I put up the rest. I worked and tried to train the horse but he didn't show anything at all."

"But Uncle Hank, with all the horses you've trained and ridden how could you make such a mistake?"

He shook his head and popped his gum.

"Well, to get on with the story, sometime later Tom's great horse, Blue, died. Tom was really busted up. He loved that horse like you would your best friend. Meeting Pat Crissman in Fat Jones's barn one day, Pat said he had to do something about Tom's moping. It seems he couldn't find a horse for Tom and things were getting serious with a heavy schedule of films coming up."

I interrupted.

"And he wanted you to sell your interest in the sorrel pony so he could give him to Tom?"

"How'd you guess? Well, I said sure. I didn't think the nag would amount to much. Maybe be a horse-double. Nothing else. Again Pat had only six bucks. But I took it thinking I was well out of losing just six bits."

My uncle was a little man, taped with TNT, who could ride anything on legs. He looked even smaller as he concluded a tale even the *Arabian Nights* couldn't top.

"Pat Crissman gave the pony to Tom. It was love at first sight. And now looking over at the sorrel I wonder if I ever had a brain in my head. Yes, he turned out to be Tony that million dollar pony you saw riding in the trailer this morning, dear nephew!"

The exploits of Tom and Tony were legendary and the bond between them as inspiring as their fame. Two near fatal accidents prove the love that bound them together in every riding moment.

On May 5, 1915, Tom Mix rode in a rodeo at the Los Angeles Stadium. Tom, on Tony as an outrider, galloped neck and neck in the chuck wagon race with two four-horse wagons. Suddenly the teams collided. Curly Eagles, driving close, leaving just enough room for a wagon to pass, tried to motion Tom not to close on him. At this instant a bridle strap broke on Eagles's leaders. There was a grinding crash and Eagles and Mix literally mixed it up, spilling Tony, pinning both against the rail. Tom and Curly were rushed unconscious from the scene. Tom suffered a broken jaw, crushed chest, fractured leg and dangerous internal injuries. Tony was miraculously unhurt.

For a week Tom Mix fought for his life.

During this crisis Tony refused to eat. He lunged at the groom who tried to enter his stall. Once a day he would take a little water.

When Tom regained consciousness and asked about Tony and was told of his behavior he demanded to be taken home. The reunion of man and horse was a tear-jerker even for the most saddle-skinned. Hand-fed by his master, Tony began eating again.

Years later in the Santa Cruz mountains of the Golden State, the script called for Tom and Tony to chase a pack of villains along a narrow trail flanked by overshadowing mountains. The villains had planted dynamite on the trail which, as Tom and Tony rode across it, would blow them sky-high.

Tom had okayed the action but when the director read it he demanded Tom use doubles for himself and Tony. Tom refused. The director asked, "Is Tony insured?"

Tom triggered back. "Your kids insured?"

"It's a little different, Tom."

"Not to me. How could money replace Tony? Besides, insuring him might be a jinx."

Tom mounted Tony, waved to the dynamiter who was going to do the detonating and galloped along the narrow trail.

As they neared the blow-up point a dust particle blew into the detonator's eye. Quickly flicking it out, his vision blurred, he pushed down the plunger thinking Tom and Tony had passed over the dynamite. It blew up just as they rode over it!

Tony lay still as death beneath Tom, a bleeding wound in his side, his legs bent, not a tremor from him as the pain mounted, not a whimper or moan.

. . . They brought a stretcher for Tom. He refused it, waiting for an attending veterinarian to administer a sedative and assure him Tony would live. Only after all possible aid had been given his little pony did Tom let them rush him to a hospital.

Most of the folks who worked with Tony considered him human. He certainly acted more like a human than a horse. He had the temperament of a big star and displayed it on the slightest provocation. One day Tony kicked up his heels and Tom, trying his best to get him into line, just walked off and left him.

Tom had just hired a three piece orchestra to "mood him up" for his thrillers and also to keep the crew and players in a happy frame of mind. As they struck up a popular tune Tony trotted over and stood listening. In a matter of minutes his tantrum was played out and the wonder horse was again making the day's shooting a bull's-eye.

I remember one day when we were working out in sandy San Fernando Valley someone forgot to bring the orchestra and Tony started acting up. From a nearby farm the prop man dug up a portable phonograph and soon Tony's ruffles were smoothed down. And forever after a phonograph went wherever Tom and Tony went.

Tony was a thoroughbred in heart only. Jet black with a white blaze on his forehead and white sox on his hind legs, he *was* Tom Mix in horse-flesh. They rode the highways and by-ways of the world. The streets of New York, Paris, London and Berlin echoed to the cheers of the crowds that had come to welcome them. The one time Tom didn't ride Tony, the most terrific cowboy in the world rode to his death in one of his high-powered cars, outside Florence, Arizona, in 1940.

Placing Duke, the Great Dane, as a footnote to the legend is not a slight. Tom loved the Dane as much as his horse. Many scenes in his epics featured Duke, and the goings-on between Duke and Tony as they tried to steal scenes from each other were in the tradition of the movies' greatest thespians.

Tom decided to settle this drama-match once and for all. He wrote and directed a film titled *Teeth.* Here is the review of that struggle of the equine against the canine.

"Tom Mix's 'toot ensemble' has been augmented by Duke, a dog. With Tony, the cowboy star's horse, the animals carry the burden of this western melodrama, built around the hero unjustly accused of murder and his faithful hound getting the goods on the real culprit.

"Every situation features the dog. Still it seems as if he knew a little too much even for a dog. He can spot a hub cap on an automobile and lift keys from a jailer's pocket. Eventually he helps the hero to rescue the girl from a forest fire—a scene effectively thrilling. Not much hard ridin' here. Mix does away with his usual exploits to give the dog a chance. And Duke can make a big bark over his performance."

Tom had this to say about this film:

"There is great rivalry between Tony, my horse, and Duke, my dog. Each feels himself the star of *Teeth.* I, myself, according to their point of view, am only one of the cast.

"There's a good deal to be said on both sides, when it comes to their relative importance. Tony, of course, claims precedence because he has already starred in his own story—*Just Tony.* He feels that Duke is nothing but a beginner.

"Duke, however, has worked with me in seventeen pictures—which is quite as good a record as Tony's.

"The truth is that they are both wonderful workers. I know that a lot of people, watching their almost human actions in *Teeth*, will think it must be the result of a lot of training. But that isn't so.

"I never have trained Tony, nor have I taught Duke any tricks. I have owned both since they were youngsters. Painstakingly at times, I have showed each just what I wanted him to do and they both have understood. When it comes to training, as understood by men who do this kind of work, Duke and Tony know nothing. They are just smart, well-behaved horse and dog.

"One day Duke sprawled his massive body on the floor of a set at the William Fox West Coast Studios, with absolutely no expression in his eyes. There seemed to him to be no reason for an expression.

"Then he saw me as I walked in. There was the wildest excitement. Duke almost deafened the bystanders with his barks. I went over and patted him, and then sat down beside him and we had our morning 'sing.' It was highly satisfactory to us, but Director Blystone and others on the set happened to think of something they had to attend to elsewhere."

Tony and Duke made personal appearances with *Teeth* during its Eastern run. Tony got the jump on Duke by having a manicure and permanent wave of his mane for their performances at the Paramount Theatre in Brooklyn. Duke, a short hair, called it sissy stuff and settled for a bath and a brush-down. But Tony, some recalled, got just a little bigger hand from the audience as they took their bows from the stage.

Tom, Tony and Duke . . . their shadows stretched from silent to sound and now television runs. And why not? They were the biggest three in talent, heart and triumph.

from NOT SO DUMB

Morris

PAUL D. BUCHANAN

*M*orris the Cat was discovered in 1966 at a Humane Society animal shelter in Hinsdale, Illinois, a southwestern suburb of Chicago. Within five years, he would become the most popular, most recognized feline in America.

Animal talent scout and manager Bob Martwick found the large orange-and-white tiger cat in a cage at the crowded shelter. As was typical for springtime in Chicago, strays were being brought in from all over northeast Illinois, and many of them would be destroyed to make room for the strays to follow. The tiger cat was scheduled next—down to eight lives in less than 20 minutes. The tiger cat caught Martwick's eye not only because of his unusual size, but also because he carried himself with a calm dignity amidst the chaos of the shelter. As Martwick took him out of the cage to have a better look at him, the cat attempted neither to flee nor to fight; it nonchalantly stood at Martwick's feet, looking him over just as Martwick was assessing the cat. Placid, even-tempered, and affectionate, he was just the sort of feline Martwick was seeking. Martwick paid the shelter five dollars, and he and the tiger cat left together. Neither life would ever be the same.

The first "9 Lives Presents Morris" commercial was filmed on location in Chicago in May of 1969 and ran for the first time in the city on May 5. The same commercial aired nationally on June 19, 1969. It was an instant hit. Morris immediately became the spokes-animal for 9 Lives cat food, and between 1969 and 1978, he starred in more than 40 commercials for the brand, produced by Leo Burnett Advertising.

While actor John Erwin provided the voice that said, "The cat that doesn't act finicky loses control of the owner," Morris clearly provided the character and the attitude. The storyline for the ads was always the same: An off-camera female voice would offer Morris some 9 Lives cat food. Morris would go into his finicky act, smugly wisecracking at his owner, refusing to show any interest in the food or to lower his facade of disdain. By the time the commercial was over, however, Morris would be face-first in the kitty dish, devouring the meal as if there were no tomorrow. Later versions of the commercial included "Doll Buggy," "Tea Party," "Girl Friend," and "Morris and Albert."

Morris's television spots were so popular that a full-time secretary named Nancy Brady was hired to handle his fan mail. In 1972 Morris was offered a starring role beside Burt Reynolds and Dyan Cannon in the detective thriller *Shamus* (1973). In July 1973, Morris was the recipient of the American Humane Association's twenty-third Annual Patsy Award as the outstanding animal star in America.

Morris's popularity continued through the seventies and into the eighties. Although the original Morris died in 1978 at the age of 19, Morris II stepped into the role, the character's popularity continued. In fact, 9 Lives ran a publicity stunt in August of 1987 announcing that Morris had thrown his hat—or perhaps, flea collar—into the ring to campaign for president of the United States. His platform included the values of "life, liberty, and the pursuit of din-din."

In the final analysis, what was it that made Morris such a charismatic figure? This typical sample from his voluminous fan mail seems to explain:

Dear Morris:

You are my hero. You have liberated the cats of America from the "soft and purry and sleepy little kitten on the best chair" cat.

We love you.

Sincerely yours,
Pussy C. Willow

from FAMOUS ANIMALS OF THE STATES

Nipper, RCA Dog

BONNIE BERGEN

This international dog symbol of the longtime RCA record label is a distinctly American story originating in England. It all started with a mutt: a bull terrier with some fox terrier genes. The death of his master caused Nipper to join Francis Barraud, who was enthralled with the old family gramophone. So was Nipper. In fact, they thought that perhaps Nipper was listening for the sound of his former master's voice!

An inspired Francis Barraud painted Nipper posed beside his old Edison-Bell cylinder phonograph and entitled it "His Master's Voice." Visitors to the Gramophone Co. Ltd., excited interest in the painting, and with some redoing, namely replacing the old phonograph with the company's new disc gramophone, it was purchased and used as a trademark in 1900 England.

On a trip to England that same year, Emile Berliner, the inventor of the disc gramophone, was so taken by the painting that upon returning to the U.S., he formally registered the trademark on May 26, 1900. Thus the delight a small dog took in the sounds of a phonograph made advertising history, beefing up the role of the dog within the high-powered, big-bucks world of national advertising. Shortly thereafter, few newspaper or magazine pages could be turned, without an appearance by man's best friend advocating a product by association or direct solicitation. That a dog's appreciation can upgrade the image of an object or person in the eyes of people is a testimony to the dog's value in our lives. This simple fact alone just may mean that people do have the ability, despite arguments to the contrary, to stretch beyond their own egos to appreciate the mind of a dog.

Almost 100 years later, Nipper look-alikes continue to participate in RCA ad campaigns to consistently stir feelings for an otherwise inanimate product line. In fact, RCA execs tell *Animal Fair* that Nipper's current successor was rescued from death row at an animal research laboratory and now travels first class, eats filet mignon, has his own limousine, and funnels his salary to save other animals from experimental research.

from ANIMAL FAIR

A Picture-Perfect Cow

RAYMOND LEE

When Gene Towne and Graham Baker started casting the 1940 version of Louisa May Alcott's classic, *Little Men,* starring Kay Francis, Jack Oakie and Jimmy Lydon, the search for a bovine to play Buttercup, the most famous cow in literature, looked like it might rival the search for the actress to play Scarlett O'Hara in *Gone With the Wind.*

At breakfast one morning Gene Towne reached for a can of milk and discovered his long-sought star, Elsie, smiling from the Borden Milk label.

Starring for two years in the Borden Milk Company exhibit at the New York 1939 World's Fair, Elsie, born to the purple, wore her crown as the nation's bucolic belle with the air of a member of the exclusive Four Hundred.

She rivaled Elsa Maxwell as a hostess, with elaborate parties at the Roosevelt Hotel for three hundred newspaper and radio magazine guests, another for three thousand at the Bovine Ball. She autographed photos for the Finnish Relief with Hendrik Willem Van Loon as her escort. At the Hotel Astor, with the Governor and Mayor of New York State and City as distinguished guests, she thrilled the Inner Circle Political Writer's Show with a brilliant performance.

Born in 1932 at Elm Hill Farm, Brookfield, Massachusetts,

of blue-blooded Isle of Jersey ancestry, Elsie was registered by the American Jersey Cattle Club as No. 998632 with the unusual name, used only among close friends, of "You'll Do Lobelia."

Her father, also having an unusual name, "You'll Do Volunteer," had contributed 266 progeny to the American bovine population and his 267th became his proudest chest-expander.

Her mother, called "Perennial Lobelia," held many awards and records for high milk production by the American Jersey Cattle Club.

Elsie combined marriage with a career in a most dexterous manner. Such famous cows as "Kingsway," "Sea Lad's Milkmaid," "Jersey Volunteer" and "You'll Do's Best" rank on the top limbs of her family tree.

Weighing 975 pounds, Elsie was one actress who didn't have to fear weight. Daily she ate forty pounds of food, which included seventeen items scientifically measured and mixed to provide nutritious milk.

Her first day on the *Little Men* set called for a scene in which Kay Francis was to milk Elsie. In a highlight of screen realism, the actors actually drank the milk massaged into the pail by Miss Francis.

Later the scenario demanded a dramatic climax for Elsie, in which she gives birth to a calf. When Towne and Baker mentioned this delicate business to Elsie's manager, he smiled back wryly. The producers hoped maybe another in their farm system could double for Elsie. The manager frowned. Elsie looked down her nose as she listened in on the conference. The manager retorted rather sharply.

"Elsie has no doubles for either acting, milking or motherhood."

Elsie and her manager exchanged coy glances as he continued.

"Only last week Elsie's personal obstetrician confirmed our suspicions—she will be a mother just about the time the picture is finished."

For once two Hollywood producers threw away their lucky rabbit's foot and patted the sides of the most cooperative cow in the world.

from NOT SO DUMB

The Champion Nobody Wanted

PEG KEHRET

$\mathcal{Z}$orro, a Great Dane/mixed-breed dog, was eight weeks old when he first came to the Humane Society. His original owner "couldn't find homes for all the puppies."

Like most puppies, Zorro was lively and lovable. Unlike most puppies, he had kennel cough and had to be confined to the medical ward until he recovered and could be put up for adoption.

Jet black, with white paws, chest, and throat and a bit of white at the tip of his tail, Zorro was a long-legged beauty. As he lost his cute puppy look, it was clear to even the most inexperienced dog person that he was going to be a mighty big dog. He had huge paws and soon weighed forty pounds.

When he recovered, he was moved to the adoption building, which has individual kennels down both sides of a wide walkway. Whenever visitors arrived, Zorro leaped eagerly against the front of the wire kennel, his long tail waving wildly. Nobody wanted to adopt such a big and rowdy dog.

Weeks went by, Zorro grew and grew, and no one chose him. Finally, when he had been at the shelter for three months, he was adopted by a family who said they wanted a big dog and were prepared to give him the care he needed. Zorro galloped away from the kennel, tugging on his leash, his tail flapping like a windshield wiper.

His happiness did not last long. Seven months later, the family returned him to the Humane Society. They said they didn't have time to exercise him, so they kept him shut in the house. Bored and restless, Zorro had begun to chew on the furniture. The family did not want a destructive dog.

By then, Zorro weighed seventy pounds, and his head reached the countertop at the adoption center. His energy level matched his size, and since he had never been taught any manners, he was now extremely hard to handle.

Of course, no one knows for sure what went through Zorro's mind as he was brought back to the Humane Society where he had already spent so much time. But he must have wondered why he was again left alone in a kennel.

Each dog who awaits adoption at the Humane Society has paperwork attached to the kennel telling his history. Every attempt is made to be honest about any problems. For example, the history might say "Does not get along with cats" or "Needs continuing treatment for ear mites." This information helps potential adopters as they try to choose a dog that will fit their lifestyle.

Now that Zorro was in the shelter a second time, his paperwork showed that he was a "returned" dog who had not worked out with his first adopting family. The paperwork also said that Zorro did not know how to obey and was known to chew—problems that would need to be corrected.

At the age of one year, Zorro, through no fault of his own, had four strikes against him: his size, his history of a failed adoption, his lack of training, and his chewing. Still, the staff hoped that some loving person would give Zorro a second chance.

Weeks passed.

No one took Zorro.

That summer, the Humane Society put on a three-week day camp for youth from troubled families. During the camp, volunteer coaches helped these young people take shelter dogs through a dog obedience class.

A Seattle woman, Megan Stanfel, offered to be a coach. Her group of campers chose to work with Zorro.

Every day for three weeks, Megan's young helpers exercised Zorro and cleaned up after him. They groomed him, brushing his black coat until it shone. They taught him to sit and stay. They decorated a special collar for him.

Zorro thrived under this attention, and he learned each lesson quickly. He no longer jumped on visitors. He knew how to walk properly on a leash.

Although Zorro was the largest dog in camp, he was never aggressive toward the other dogs or to any of the people in the program. The campers nicknamed him "the Gentle Giant."

Megan and her young workers knew that they were helping Zorro become more adoptable. They groomed him especially well on Fridays so that he would look his best over the weekend, when most adoptions take place. Despite their efforts, Zorro stayed at the shelter.

On the final day of camp, the dogs "graduated." Zorro wore his new collar and marched in to the music "Pomp and Circumstance." The camp's obedience trainers voted him "Most Cooperative Dog."

News photographers attended the graduation, and Megan urged them to photograph Zorro. She hoped someone would see his picture and fall in love with this handsome animal whose good manners now matched his good looks. But the photographers said black dogs are harder to photograph than light-colored ones; once again, Zorro was not selected.

Megan attached a note to the paperwork on Zorro's kennel, saying how well he had worked with children during the summer camp and how quickly he had learned his obedience lessons. She mentioned that he was voted Most Cooperative Dog and that he got along with all the other dogs in camp.

Although the camp was over, Megan continued to volunteer at the Humane Society. Each time she came, she went first to Zorro's kennel, hoping he would not be there. He always was.

One day Megan gave him a bath so he would look and smell his best. But a month went by, and still Zorro had no family.

Each year, the Humane Society's main fund-raiser is an event called "Tuxes and Tails." This consists of an auction and a celebrity/pet fashion show where sports stars, radio and television personalities, and other celebrities model the latest fashions. As the celebrities walk down the runway, each is accompanied by a dog. Some bring their own dogs; most use dogs from the shelter.

Tuxes and Tails always gets wide media coverage, so Megan arranged for Zorro to be in the show. Maybe someone in the audience or watching news clips on TV would want to adopt him. She practiced walking with him, helping him remember how to act on a leash.

The celebrity wore a black tuxedo; Zorro wore a crisp white bow tie—plus his usual black fur coat and white bib. Zorro pranced down the runway, tail wagging. The audience applauded loudly for the handsome pair—but nobody asked to adopt Zorro.

Megan and her husband, Ken, discussed adopting Zorro themselves. They already had two dogs. Buddy, a mix of German shepherd, Lab, and husky, had a seizure disorder and needed special medical care. Lester, a beagle/basset mix, had been abused before Megan and Ken found him abandoned in a park, and he was still fearful of new situations.

Megan and Ken worried that bringing a huge, rambunctious dog like Zorro into their home would not be fair to Buddy and Lester. They weren't sure it would be fair to Zorro, either.

"Zorro is so special," Megan told Ken. "He deserves to be the only dog in a loving family—not the third dog."

Megan often cried with frustration when she arrived at the shelter and found Zorro still there. She always took him to the outdoor courtyard for exercise. Other volunteers exercised him, too, but these brief encounters were not enough for such a large and lively dog.

As weeks became months and Zorro remained in the kennel, he slipped back into his old habits. Without regular practice, he forgot the obedience lessons he had learned. Zorro became hard to handle again.

As the days slid past, Zorro gradually withdrew. He was always glad to see Megan, but other volunteers could no longer coax him out of the kennel. Zorro was quickly becoming unadoptable. If he quit interacting with people, he would have to be euthanized.

Finally Megan could not stand to watch Zorro deteriorate any longer. She and Ken agreed to give Zorro the only chance he would get; they adopted him themselves.

While Ken drove, Megan sat in the back seat with Zorro. All

the way home, he licked her hands as his tail beat against the car window. Happy sounds bubbled from his throat, and he physically shook with joy.

"I promise you," Megan told him, "that you will never, ever go back to the Humane Society."

At home, Buddy and Lester met the newcomer. They sniffed Zorro, and Zorro sniffed them. Tails wagged. Low-slung Lester walked under Zorro and stood there; when Zorro jumped out of the way, Lester walked under him again. Buddy sat down to watch. It quickly became a game, and both dogs seemed happy to have a new playmate.

When Megan and Ken took Zorro inside, he calmly followed them through the house, carefully keeping his tail under control.

"Zorro was absolutely no trouble," Megan says. "We expected it to be a huge adjustment for all of us. Instead, he fit right in. Although his head reaches the kitchen counter, he has never tried to take food. He is gentle with Lester and Buddy, and he loves his daily walks in the park."

Megan enrolled Zorro in a novice obedience class. He did so well that she continued with an advanced class.

One day the obedience instructor invited Megan and Zorro to attend a Flyball competition.

"A what?" Megan said.

"Flyball. It's a dog relay race. There are two teams of four dogs each. When the starter says 'Go!' the lead dog on each team races down a lane, jumping across four hurdles, and triggers a ball box with his paw. That releases a tennis ball. The dog catches the ball, makes a quick U-turn, and carries the ball back over the hurdles to the starting line. As soon as he gives the ball to his handler, the second dog on the team starts off.

The race keeps going until all four dogs are finished. The team that's fastest wins."

Curious, Megan went to watch a Flyball race. She saw dogs of all sizes and breeds, including mixed breeds like Zorro, playing Flyball. The dogs and the people all seemed to be having fun. The dogs waited eagerly for their turns, some of them barking with excited anticipation.

Thinking that Flyball would provide good exercise for Zorro, Megan taught him the Flyball routine. He loved running fast and going over the jumps. He quickly caught on how to release the tennis ball from the box, and he always raced back to Megan with it, eager to get her approval and a treat. Before long, he did so well that he was invited to compete.

Right from the start, Zorro was good at Flyball. Soon he won a Flyball title and then another and then a third. He won ribbons and medals.

He was asked to join the Puget Sound Flyers, a Flyball demonstration team whose purpose is entertainment rather than racing. Zorro's team performs at half-time during many sporting events.

Megan took him to do shows at the University of Washington during basketball and soccer games. They traveled to Vancouver, British Columbia, in Canada, where they were the special guests of the Vancouver Grizzlies, a National Basketball Association team.

Zorro was classified as an "entertainer" as he crossed the border into Canada. After the Flyball performance, the Grizzlies provided Megan and Zorro with their own hotel suite for the night. It was definitely more luxurious than a kennel at the Humane Society!

"People tell me how lucky Zorro is that I adopted him,"

Megan says. "But I am the lucky one. He has enriched my life in so many ways."

Megan used to take the bus to the Humane Society because she didn't drive. After Zorro began Flyball competitions, Megan learned to drive and got her own car so that she could transport Zorro to his meets.

The obedience instructor who taught Zorro's classes saw the expert way Megan handled this large dog and offered her a part-time job. Megan now teaches obedience classes. Zorro sometimes goes along to demonstrate the proper methods. Zorro also took the necessary training to qualify as a therapy dog so Megan can take him to visit hospitalized children. Even the sickest children smile when they pet big, friendly Zorro.

Zorro's Flyball team was invited to provide the half-time entertainment at a Seattle Sonics basketball game. Each dog on the Puget Sound Flyers wore a new auburn-and-gold coat. With his black fur and golden eyes, Zorro looked particularly handsome.

The Key Arena in Seattle, where the Sonics play, was sold out that night, and when Zorro finished his routine, the crowd gave him a standing ovation.

As the applause echoed from the rafters, Megan stood with tears in her eyes. She thought of all the lonely months Zorro spent in the Humane Society shelter—months when no one wanted him.

Since then, Zorro has demonstrated Flyball at a New Jersey Nets game at the Meadowlands in East Brunswick, New Jersey; at a Cavaliers game in Cleveland, Ohio; and at New York Knicks games in Madison Square Garden in New York City. His team donates any profits from performance fees to animal welfare organizations or uses the money to buy new equipment and coats for the dogs. The team also does many free shows for charities, senior centers, and the University of Washington.

Whether it's a small group or a crowd of thousands, the response is always the same: everyone cheers for Zorro, the shelter dog who became a champion.

from SHELTER DOGS

LOVE REMEMBERED

_____

"My goal in life is to become as wonderful as my dog thinks I am."

TOBY AND EILEEN GREEN

_____

*S*ometimes an animal becomes famous for doing what animals do best—making people happy. Whether they lie at our feet as we work, or greet us as if we're the most important person in the world, or help us to grow from happy-go-lucky child to caring adult, they make us better human beings. They bring out what God put into us.

A President's Pup

ROY ROWAN AND BROOKE JANIS

Warren Harding once said, "I am not fit for this office and should never have been here." And he probably was right. Yet his triumph by a huge majority in 1920 signified an end of the progressive era and a moratorium on reform. "Return to Normalcy" had been his Republican campaign theme. A handsome man who was devoted to his dogs, this president relied on canines to abet his campaign and later to help lead him out of a political morass.

The Hardings came to the White House with an English bulldog named Oh Boy. He was a sickly little creature and soon died. But his replacement, the airedale Laddie Boy—or Caswell Laddie Boy, his full pedigree name—became the President's constant companion and a White House celebrity.

Laddie Boy knew the President by his first name. First Lady Florence Harding would hand the dog the morning newspaper and say, "Take this to Warren." Then with the rolled-up paper clenched in his teeth, the dog would trot off to find his master. Laddie Boy would also participate in the President's favorite pastime, happily retrieving his golf balls out on the White House lawn.

This animal, unlike all the presidential dogs before him, got involved in the workings of the government. Not only did he have his own hand-carved cabinet chair and sit in on high-level meetings, he was also often on the front steps of the White House to greet official delegations. Although he was so well known to reporters that they frequently quoted him in mock interviews, Laddie Boy failed to deflect attention from the excesses that soon engulfed the Harding administration—scandals and payoffs that were part of Harding's "Spoils System."

Once Harding even tried to use a fictitious correspondence between Laddie Boy and a vaudeville dog named Tiger to defend his loyalty to several presidential appointees who turned out to be defrauding the government. Published in a political magazine called *The National,* a letter from Tiger commended Laddie Boy for sticking by his master through thick and thin. Laddie Boy then replied that both man and dog could be undone by people who used friendship for their personal gain. Harding's airedale was thus echoing the anguish of his beleaguered master. . . .

Despondent and in poor health, the President and his wife took off in 1923 on a cross-country speaking tour ending in Alaska. He fell ill on the way home and died in San Francisco. Back in the White House, Laddie Boy was said to have sensed something was wrong and howled for three days just prior to the President's death.

To avoid the pain of being constantly reminded of her late husband, the First Lady gave Laddie Boy away to the Secret Service agent who had guarded them on the fateful trip to Alaska. Though Harding served barely two years and was one of the country's least successful chief executives, his death produced an outpouring of national grief. As a result, the Newsboys Association decided to present Mrs. Harding with a remembrance of the President's famous dog. Some nineteen thousand members each chipped in one penny to be melted down and cast into a statue of Laddie Boy. Unfortunately she, too, died before sculptor Bashka Paeff completed the piece, which now resides in the Smithsonian.

from FIRST DOGS

The World's Most-Traveled Dog

LEILA DORNAK

Outside, a bitter wind whipped around the corners of buildings, and the wind chill factor dipped to a frigid low. Albany, New York, was one of the coldest spots in the nation that winter night in 1888.

Shivering in the icy gusts of wind, a small dog roamed the dark streets of the town, seeking shelter. Everywhere doors were tightly closed against the wintry blasts. The dog, too cold to even notice the pains of hunger that gnawed at his stomach, came at last to the post office. Here he found an opening, a place he could be protected from the cold breath of Mother Nature.

Inside, a pile of empty mail sacks looked like heaven to him. He gratefully crept into their midst, sinking down into a pocket of softness. His tired bones eventually began to warm and he fell into exhausted sleep.

Next morning, postal clerks arriving to begin their day's work found him still there. No longer quite as cold, but much hungrier, the scrawny mutt aroused their sympathy. They couldn't find it in their hearts to send him back out into the streets to fend for himself. Instead, they shared their lunch with him and allowed him to stay in the post office.

Days passed and no owner showed up to claim the little stray. The postal workers had quickly grown fond of him. They cleaned him up and made an official place for him to sleep—in the corner of the office. And, so that he need no longer be an unknown wanderer in the cold, dark streets, they named him "Owney."

Little did they dream then of the adventures and fame their small, mousy brown dog would have in the years to follow. For Owney was destined to become a world traveler, recognized and welcomed by postal workers everywhere.

Unlike the pony of the Pony Express and the eagle of today's U.S. Postal Service, Owney became a real, live mascot of the United States mail.

After the first bitterly cold night when he found shelter in the Albany post office, Owney looked on mail bags as his special haven. Wherever he found a mail sack was home to him. He especially liked riding on top of the pouches when the mail was taken to the train depot in horse-drawn wagons.

One day he watched with bright-eyed interest as the pouches were transferred from the wagon to the train. The crew of postal workers called him aboard with them, and the friendly little dog accepted the invitation. He followed his beloved mail sacks onto the Railway Post Office mail car and made himself at home.

That first train ride with the U.S. Mail took him to New York City. And this was only the beginning. Owney soon endeared himself to all the Railway Post Office crews, and they were glad to have him accompany them on their runs.

Trains were a principal mode of mail transportation in Owney's day, and he spent weeks at a time on the road, wandering farther and farther from his original postal home. He traveled to so many cities that the Albany post office workers were afraid he might get lost. They fitted him with a collar tagged with his name and address. On it, they asked that postal clerks in places he visited add tags to show that Owney had been there.

Owney collected those tags for almost ten years. He had them from all over the United States, from Alaska, from Canada, from Mexico. Finally there were so many that his collar could no longer hold them all. So the postmaster general ordered a special jacket for Owney to wear with all his tags attached. Owney wore it proudly as he set out on even greater adventures.

Just as he followed mail sacks aboard a train in Albany, so he followed them aboard a steamer bound for the Orient. He set out from Tacoma, Washington, and under the personal care of the ship's captain, arrived safely in Japan. There he was introduced to the emperor who added a tag to Owney's jacket. His next stop was China, and on the homeward journey he collected medals in Hong Kong, Singapore, Algiers, and Port Said. Home again, he disembarked in New York City, hopped aboard a Railway Post Office and headed back to Tacoma. Owney had traveled all the way around the world in 132 days—good reason for his reputation as "The World's Most-Traveled Dog."

Owney's life was filled with adventures. His travels abounded with escapades worthy of any hero of the roads. Once he was taken prisoner and held captive on a chain in a logging camp. The president of the railroad, determined to free him, stopped a train and dispatched a rescue unit. Owney was brought triumphantly "home" to the mail car where he was, once again, able to sleep on his cherished mail bags.

Another adventure put him on the wrong side of the law in

Canada. That time, his Albany friends took up a collection in the office and bailed him out.

After nearly ten years of Owney's adventurous feats, the post office department felt the time had come for him to settle down. By then he had only one good eye and could eat nothing but soft food. He deserved quiet, relaxation and good care for the rest of his days. They planned a retirement party in San Francisco. Owney, used to public appearances at dog shows, had a fine time at the celebration. He walked on stage, wearing his jacket with its one thousand and seventeen medals, before an audience of wildly cheering Railway Post Office clerks from all over the United States.

After the party Owney returned to Albany with his special friends, the clerks who had found him that first cold winter day. There he was supposed to stay and enjoy his retirement.

But Owney had a strong streak of independence. He also had a mind of his own. One of the tags he wore bore this poem:

> Only one Owney,
> And this is he;
> The dog is a loney,
> So let him be.

It described him well. Owney had no intention of being confined to one place when the whole world was full of mysteries, adventures and mail bags. He slipped away one day and set off on one final trail. He got as far as Toledo, Ohio. There he died as he had lived, on the road with postal friends around him. The little Globe Trotter would travel no more; his rambling days were done. Or were they?

Owney never followed his mail bags onto a plane, but his was a high-flying spirit. It isn't hard to imagine him still perched atop stacks of mail pouches winging their way to Zanzibar or Timbuktu. As long as mail carriers transport mail in sacks, the memory of Owney will follow them, medals jingling as he bounces along in search of new adventures.

from OUR BEST FRIENDS

The Changing Seasons

WILLIE MORRIS

"Time, he is a tricky fellow," Lewis Carroll said. Old Skip had come to us when I was nine years old; by the time I entered high school, I was fourteen and he was four. If, as the authorities often declare, a dog's life in relation to a human being's can be calculated by seven human years to his one, then Skip was twenty-eight when I was fourteen. This is all too confusing, however, and I intend not to place much stock in it: my memories of Skip move in and out and around in time anyway, from my grade school years through junior high and high school and beyond, which is likely as it should be, because if the existence of all creatures is a continuum, there is still plenty of room to weave and backtrack and drift and glide. Life is indeed a confluence, but seldom a steady one, and embraces forever the changing seasons.

Autumn: Our region of America never had the great flamboyant, bursting beauty of northern autumns, but there was a languor to our Octobers and Novembers, especially in the dry falls when the foliage was so profound and varied, and the very landscape itself would be imbued with a golden, poignant sheen.

One Saturday during the autumn I woke up quite early to take full advantage of the fresh, free Saturday ambiance, and in such a disposition *I* woke up *Skip* rather than the reverse, and we lounged around in bed for a few more minutes as I considered the day's unique possibilities. My room was quite small but nonetheless contained an unusual number of interesting items: colorful pennants from a dozen colleges; the German helmet and belt hanging from nails on the wall; horns from a dead cow; a photograph of the 1946 St. Louis Cardinals; my father's old baseball glove; a bookcase with books by Mark Twain, Zane Grey, Dickens, and Poe; the rattlers from the rattlesnake I had killed in the woods; four chunks of petrified mud picked up along ancient creekbeds; and various photographs of Skip with Rivers Applewhite, the other boys, the bulldog Buck with whom he had shared the first prize in the dog contest, and myself.

Lying there in bed with Skip beside me, I gingerly recalled the major events of the day before. After school Friday he had been waiting for me at his appointed place on the boulevard. We immediately went home and got my bicycle and rushed out to the black high school football field to see the Black Panthers play a game and to imbibe the lavish flair of their players and fans. They played in the discarded uniforms of our high school, so that their school colors were the same as ours, and they even played the same towns up in the Delta that our high school did. Skip and I normally sat on the sidelines next to the cheering section, but one afternoon the referee asked me to carry one of the first-down markers, and Skip followed closely beside me during that entire game as I fulfilled these official responsibilities. Next I conjured the scenes from last night's white high school game, which Skip, Peewee, and I had watched from the end-zone bleachers, and the infectious undercurrent of excitement there, for on Fridays in the fall you could

almost feel this tension in the atmosphere, the unreserved rev-
erence for the game itself, the awesome thuds of big old boys
running headlong into each other, the off-key marching bands,
the cheerleaders making pyramids of flesh, while all through
this pandemonium the spectators slapped at the manifold
Delta bugs attracted from the nearby swamp-bottoms by the
lights of the stadium.

At about nine o'clock I got dressed in a pair of blue jeans,
tennis shoes, a white T-shirt, and a green baseball cap with a *Y*
on it. Skip and I ate some raisin bran in the kitchen; then I led
him outside for a lengthy session of retrieving sticks. It was
Indian summer and everything—the earth and the trees,
touched by the airy sunshine—was the lazy golden-brown of
that sad and lovely time; there was the faint presence of smoke
everywhere, and the smell of leaves burning, and sounds and
their echoes carried a long, long way. Wherever you looked
there was a truckload of raw cotton coming in for ginning;
along the country roads and even the paved avenues in town
you could see the white cotton bolls that had fallen to the
ground. The county fair was on, and every night that week we
had taken in the 4-H exhibits—the vegetables, and the bottled
preserves of all the shades of the rainbow, and the pumpkins,
and the great slabs of meat. How Skip loved those county fairs!
He strolled the grounds with the other boys and me in a spirit
of fine titillation, ate the cotton candy Rivers Applewhite gave
him, and waited impatiently while we took the carnival rides. I
had tried to get the man who ran the Ferris wheel to let him go
on it with us, but he was not sympathetic. "This contraption
ain't no place for a dog."

In our backyard on this Saturday morning Skip was by now
a little tired out from his exertions, and it was time to consult

with Henjie. I went into the house and told the telephone oper-
ator his number (it was 27; mine was 243; my father's office
was 1). When Henjie answered the phone, I wanted to know if
everyone was coming to the football field, and he said they
would all be there at ten; we had stopped going to the Saturday
Kiddie Matinee when the war ended and we felt we had out-
grown it anyway. I fiddled around with the radio awhile, and
read the *Memphis Commercial Appeal* for the football scores;
then I got on my bicycle and headed up the street toward the
football stadium, with Skip following, stopping every so often
for him to examine a dead frog or some other lifeless object or
to greet an old lady.

When he and I reached the field, the same site at which he
had earlier set the world record for fox terriers, we ran a few
wind sprints, then examined the cleat marks that had been
made in the turf the night before by our high school heroes.
Three thousand people had been in these grandstands and the
bleachers just a few hours ago! I did a pantomime of a forty-
three-yard scoring play, dodging Skip and the imagined tacklers
on last night's exact route to glory. Then the boys showed up,
including Peewee with his official Southeastern Conference
football with the dangling lace for Skip to carry in his mouth on
his running plays, and we chose up sides and played a brisk
brand of tackle until the twelve o'clock whistle blew at the
sawmill. The only injuries on this day were to Peewee's big toe,
which he claimed he sprained when tripping on a cleat mark,
and to Henjie's head, which he said Big Boy had mistaken
for the football. The final score was 86–69, my team over
Muttonhead's.

The afternoon held many possibilities, but this one began
with fried chicken and biscuits and other delicacies at Bubba's

house, for his mother's refrigerator contained a plethora of riches mournfully absent from the one at my house, and then an interlude listening to the Ole Miss or State football game on the radio, because there has always been a religiosity to college football in our region, and Saturday is the holy day. After that we rode our bicycles to Main Street to see the latest Boston Blackie movie, then returned to my house to get our DeSoto and take a spin around town, from the telegraph shack at the end of Main Street to the Country Club at the rim of the Delta. Only a scant minority of its citizens had never seen Skip behind the steering wheel, but we managed to locate a little store on Brickyard Hill which was virgin territory, and the inevitable old man shouted: *"Look at that ol' dog drivin' a car!"* Then we proceeded to Henjie's house to listen to the college football results on the radio. We lounged on his front porch and watched the leaves drift from the oak trees and listened indolently to the scores—first those of the little schools in the East like Williams and Colby and Amherst and Niagara, or Allegheny and Susquehanna and King's Point and Lafayette; then the Ivy League scores, which were just exercises; on to the big midwestern and southern ones that really mattered—moving slowly across the country like a great roll call of America.

After that Skip and I took off for home, walking down the hills toward the quiet flat streets, and making it just in time for hamburgers and french fries. After supper I turned on the lamp in the front yard and put the portable radio on the porch, tuning it to the LSU game from Tiger Stadium in Baton Rouge, and Skip and I played football again by ourselves, I making up the whole game to the accompanying din of the thousands from the radio, racing ninety-five yards for fictitious touchdowns before seventy-five thousand cheering fanatics, intercepting enemy passes in the dying seconds of the fourth quarter, kicking forty-six-yard field goals against thirty-mile-an-hour winds. By now it had been a long autumn Saturday. Old Skip and I stretched out on the cool, wet grass. I used the football for a pillow and he lay down beside me and we gazed up at the stars until it was time to go in to bed.

In remembering moments such as these, I retain the sad-sweet reflection of being an only child and having a loyal and loving dog, for in the struggles of life, of the dangers, toils, and snares of my childhood hymns, loyalty and love are the best things of all, and the most lasting, and that is what Old Skip taught me that I carry with me now.

from MY DOG SKIP

The Wisest One

ENOS MILLS

(Editor's Note: Enos Mills, an early activist on behalf of wilderness preservation, was well known for his books and lectures—and for Scotch, the dog who accompanied him on many of his remarkable explorations.)

*M*any of Scotch's actions were beyond the scope of instinct. One day, when still young, he mastered a new situation by the use of his wits. While he was alone at the house, some frightened cattle smashed a fence about a quarter of a mile away and broke into the pasture. He was after them in an instant. From a mountain-side ledge above, I watched proceedings with a glass. The cattle were evidently excited by the smell of some animal and did not drive well. Scotch ignored the two pasture gates, which were closed, and endeavored to hurry the cattle out through the break through which they had entered. After energetic encouragement, all but one went flying out through the break. This one alternated between stupidly running back and forth along the fence and trying to gore Scotch. Twice the animal had run into a corner by one of the gates, and his starting for the corner the third time apparently gave Scotch an idea. He stopped heeling, raced for the gate, and, leaping up, bit at the handle of the sliding wooden bar that secured it.

He repeated this biting and tearing at the handle until the bar slid and the gate swung open. After chasing the animal through, he lay down by the gate.

When I came into view he attracted my attention with sharp barks and showed great delight when I closed the gate. After this, he led me to the break in the fence and then lay down. Though I looked at him and asked, "What do you want done here?" he pretended not to hear. That was none of his business!

He had much more individuality than most dogs. His reserve force and initiative usually enabled him to find a way and succeed with situations which could not be mastered in his old way. The gate-opening was one of the many incidents in which these traits brought triumph.

One of his most remarkable achievements was the mastering of a number of cunning coyotes which were persistent in annoying him and willing to make an opportunity to kill him. In a sunny place close to the cabin, the coyotes one autumn frequently collected for a howling concert. This irritated Scotch, and he generally chased the howlers into the woods. Now and then he lay down on their yelping-grounds to prevent their prompt return. After a time these wily little wolves adopted tantalizing tactics, and one day, while Scotch was chasing the pack, a lame coyote made a detour and came behind him. In the shelter of a willow-clump the coyote broke out in a maddening Babel of yelps and howls. Scotch instantly turned back to suppress him. While he was thus busy, the entire pack doubled back into the open and taunted Scotch with attitude and howls.

Twice did the pack repeat these annoying, defying tactics. This serious situation put Scotch on his mettle. One night he went down the mountain to a ranch-house fifteen miles away.

For the first time he was gone all night. The next morning I was astonished to find another collie in Scotch's bed. Scotch was in a state of worried suspense until I welcomed the stranger; then he was most gleeful. This move on his part told plainly that he was planning something still more startling. Indeed he was, but never did I suspect what this move was to be.

That day, at the first howl of the coyotes, I rushed out to see if the visiting collie would assist Scotch. There were the coyotes in groups of two and three, yelping, howling, and watching. Both dogs were missing, but presently they came into view, cautiously approaching the coyotes from behind a screen of bushes. Suddenly the visiting collie dashed out upon them. At the same instant Scotch leaped into a willow-clump and crouched down; it was by this clump that the lame coyote had each time come to howl behind Scotch.

While the visiting collie was driving the pack, the lame coyote again came out to make his sneaking flank movement. As he rounded the willow-clump Scotch leaped upon him. Instantly the other dog raced back, and both dogs fell fiercely upon the coyote. Though lame, he was powerful, and finally shook the dogs off and escaped to the woods, but he was badly wounded and bleeding freely. The pack fled and came no more to howl near the cabin.

At bedtime, when I went out to see the dogs, both were away. Their tracks in the road showed that Scotch had accompanied the neighboring collie at least part of the way home.

On rare occasions Scotch was allowed to go with visitors into the woods or up the mountain-side. However, he was allowed to accompany only those who appreciated the companionship and the intelligence of a noble dog or who might need him to show the way home.

One day a young woman from Michigan came along and wanted to climb Long's Peak alone and without a guide. I agreed to consent to her wish if she would take Scotch with her and would also first climb one of the lesser peaks on a stormy day, unaided. This climbing the young woman did, and by so doing convinced me that she had a keen sense of direction and an abundance of strength, for the day was a stormy one and the peak was completely befogged with clouds. After this there was nothing for me to do but to allow her to climb Long's Peak.

Just as she was starting for Long's Peak that cool September morning, I called Scotch and said to him: "Scotch, go with this young woman up Long's Peak. Keep her on the trail, take good care of her, and stay with her until she returns!" Scotch gave a few barks of satisfaction and started with the young woman up the trail, carrying himself in a manner which indicated that he was both honored and pleased. I felt that the strength and alertness of the young woman, when combined with the faithfulness and watchfulness of Scotch, would make the ascent a success, for the dog knew the trail as well as any guide.

The young woman climbed swiftly until she reached the rocky alpine moorlands above timber-line. Here she lingered long to enjoy the magnificent scenery and the brilliant flowers. It was late in the afternoon when she arrived at the summit of the Peak. After she had spent a little time there, resting and absorbing the beauty and grandeur of the scene, she started to return. She had not gone far when clouds and darkness came on, and on a slope of slide rock she turned aside from the trail.

Scotch had minded his own affairs and enjoyed himself in his own way all day long. Most of the time he had followed her

closely, apparently indifferent to what happened. But the instant the young woman left the trail and started off in the
wrong direction, he sprang ahead and took the lead with an
alert, aggressive air. The way in which he did this should have
suggested to her that he knew what he was about, but she did
not appreciate this fact. She thought he had become weary
and wanted to run away from her, so she called him back.
Again she started in the wrong direction. This time Scotch got
in front of her and refused to move. She pushed him out of the
way. Once more he started off in the right direction and this
time she scolded him and reminded him that his master had
told him to stay with her. Scotch dropped his ears, fell in behind her, and followed meekly in her steps. He had tried to
carry out the first part of his master's orders; now he was re-
signed to the second part of them.

After going a short distance, the young woman realized
that she had lost her trail but it never occurred to her that she
had only to let Scotch have his way and he would lead her
safely home. However, she had the good sense to stop where
she was. And there, among the crags, by the stained remnants
of winter's snow, thirteen thousand feet above sea-level, she
knew she must pass the night. The wind blew a gale and the
alpine brooklet turned to ice, while, in the lee of a crag, shivering with cold and hugging Scotch tight, she lay down to wait
for daylight.

When darkness had come that evening and the young
woman had not returned, I sent a rescue party of four guides
up the Peak. They suffered much from cold as they vainly
searched among the crags through the dark hours of the windy
night. Just at sunrise one of the guides found her. She was
almost exhausted, but was still hugging Scotch tightly and only

her fingers were frostbitten. The guide gave her wraps and food and drink, and started with her down the trail. And Scotch? Oh, as soon as the guide appeared he left her and started home for breakfast. Scotch saved this young woman's life by staying with her through the long, cold night. She appreciated the fact, and was quick to admit that if she had allowed the dog to have his own way about the trail she would have had no trouble.

from THE STORY OF SCOTCH

Devotion

PETER C. JONES AND LISA MacDONALD

Silverton, Oregon—Loyalty knows no bounds. When Bobbie, a Scottish collie mix, was separated from his family on a trip to Indiana, he spent the next six months traveling three thousand miles cross country to return home.

Witnesses who helped recreate the journey determined that the faithful dog had battled the rapids of the White River, crossed the Mississippi and the Rockies and even walked out on a family that wanted to adopt him. Increasingly weary, with the pads of his paws worn to the bone, Bobbie accepted help for his injuries in Portland, then took to the road for the final leg of his journey to Silverton.

To the astonishment of his family, he returned home. The exhausted dog lived long enough to enjoy his homecoming, but the journey had taken its toll. Bobbie died at the tender age of six with the full and complete knowledge that "there's no place like home." A simple memorial in Portland honors this devoted dog whose fame spread across the nation back in 1923 and whose legend lives on.

from HERO DOGS

Red Dog Retriever

DAVID HENDERSON

I have always taken pride in being known as a storyteller. Here at 80, and in an era of cyberspace, whatever that is, I may be one of the last to pass on verbally the tales told to me by my father, and his before him. But before time calls the coda on this life, I need to record the story of the great red dog. And what she did to deserve it.

Actually, it was told to me many times by my dad, her heroics having occurred shortly before I was born. But if you keep reading, you'll see why I have cause for gratitude.

"Once upon a time," he'd say, "there was a boy who lived by the sea." And, of course, I'd know that boy was my dad. Then he'd tell how he grew up in the village of Chester on the North Carolina coast. Actually, it faced on Core Sound, named for the Core Indian tribe found there by the first English colonists. Every Chesterman was a waterman, making a living fishing or guiding for ducks and geese in season. And many a time, out of season as well, back in the day of market hunters.

But also, every man at one time or another in his life, served in the U.S. Life-Saving Service (later the U.S. Coast Guards). For just south lay the famous Cape Lookout, and the Core Banks and Lookout shoals that were almost as deadly to shipping as the "graveyard of the Atlantic" further north at

Cape Hatteras. And a surfman received $65 a month, cash, for the ten danger months, although he had to pay for his uniform and keep. Still, this was far better than most residents of Carteret County earned at the turn of the century. And my Dad, about twenty in the early 1900's, was a surfman in District 6.

This, though, is the story of a dog, and how she came to be a part of the crew.

Dad said that he had lived for two winters up near the Virginia line, guiding for rich Northerners who had built hunting lodges at Knott's Island, Corolla, and Pine Island. A Mr. Sears lived at Water Lily on Currituck Sound and hired out to outfit, which meant he had skiffs and furnished guides. Unlike most of the Currituck folks, Mr. Sears raised and kept retrievers. His were the biggest, bulkiest, and best in the region, and they were all Chesapeakes. "Tougher 'n whitleather," Dad said.

About the end of the Season in 1908 or '09, Sears had a reservation for hunters from Philadelphia and persuaded Dad to stay and guide. When the hunters cancelled, Mr. Sears said he didn't have the money to pay Dad, but, "maybe you'll feel better if you take one of Sheila's pups." Now there was nothing an Atlantic Coast guide would rather have than one of the Sear's Chessies, so a bargain was struck.

In the litter was a gyp that stood out from the rest because, instead of the chocolate brown of the bitch and the dog, this little one was almost RED. Just about the color of a chow or redbone hound. She was first to come out of the box, and Dad promptly put the eight-week-old youngster in the pocket of his hunting coat. And so, off south to Chester, and the girl Dad pined for—my mother to be. He named the pup "Rose," after mother, but nobody ever called her anything but "Red."

By the beginning of the following season she, with her inherited genes, weighed almost seventy pounds, and was destined at her peak (no pun intended) to tip the scales at well over a hundred. Dad said she was a natural retriever, having had a battering from an old crippled gander early on, and thereafter putting her foot on the head of every bird before picking up and returning. And she was the strongest swimmer in the community. Early on, because there were few retrievers locally, nobody knew just how much she was a mistress of the sea.

My Uncle Tom Fulcher, my mother's youngest brother, was just a boy when Dad brought Rose home. He was an old man when last I talked to him. Fulcher is a name well remembered in what are locally known as the "Straights Settlements," that series of fishing villages running north from the trading town of Beaufort, through Davis and Stacy and to Cedar Island, where a ferry ran to Portsmouth Island. Uncle Tom had operated the ferry and knew everybody within twenty miles.

I pressed him to tell me what he remembered about how things were, and especially about Rose that everybody called Red. Uncle Tom remembered that she would retrieve anything smaller than she was. Once there was a fire in the village, a residence belonging to some folks named Sawyer. He was the local butcher. The old house had withstood twenty hurricanes in its lifetime, but a careless hand with the kerosene heater spoiled that record in a trice.

Now in the days when there was no piped water and everyone relied on a dug well, there wasn't really much that could be done to quench a house fire. The crossroads had a "pumper" pulled by hand, and when a hose was tossed in a well, two volunteers pushed-pulled a rocking handle that forced water up from the well—at least until the well went dry.

At the Sawyer's, twenty or so neighbors were rushing around and Uncle Tom and Zeke Mitchell were manning the pump, but throwing very little water. Then it was that Mrs. Sawyer began screaming, asking who had seen little Danny, her two-year-old. She was fighting to go back into the burning house, holding the child's jacket which she had grabbed on her way to safety.

Uncle Tom said Dad came up about then and, sensing the peril the child might be in, snatched the child's clothing from the panicky mother and, sticking it under Red's nose, said "fetch." Now we aren't talking about bloodhounds, nor trained retrievers—just a young duck dog. Uncle Tom said he could have made the story really exciting if he had told me Red jumped through ten foot flames to make a rescue. The truth was, Red bored in under the smoke on the bedroom side of the house, found a retrievable that smelled like what Dad had been holding and, picking the youngster up by his britches, retrieved him to hand. Dad's hand, that is.

If nothing had, up until that time, made Red something special in the community, the saving of Danny Sawyer certainly did. Of course there was no medal, no reward, just a hug from Mrs. Sawyer and, next butchering, Mr. Sawyer dropped by Dad's with a shank bone.

Dad guided frequently when not registered as a surfman or part-time surfman. Some of the people he'd guided for on Currituck followed him south, staying at Beaufort, or with boarding houses at Marshallberg, or Davis or a crossroad later named "Otway" for an ancestor of one of Dad's clients. Mr. Clarence Otway came from shipping in New York City, and frequently brought with him a fellow shipper, a Mr. Carter, and Otway's nephew, Andrew. Nobody locally would guide if

Andrew was in the party because of his attitude, which to put on the best face, was simply "snotty." Once, however, when money was short, Mr. Otway asked Dad to make an exception and to take his party.

Dad said that he had access to a stilt blind in the sound, and finally agreed to take the three Northerners for the day. Shooting was good, and they were approaching the limits when Red brought in a canvasback and, shaking herself free of ice water, attempted to retrieve as always directly to Dad. Unfortunately, he told me, the dog had to bypass Andrew, who reached out for the bird. She would not drop. Whereupon, Andrew slapped her across the face. That was a mistake of the first order.

Now the first rule of guiding is restraint where paying clients are concerned, but Dad said he simply slapped Andrew, knocking him flat, and stood on his gun hand, still locked around the shotgun. Andrew got up shouting that he was getting a warrant for assault "as soon as I get to town." It was then that Mr. O, standing only about five feet six, quietly said to his kinsman, "That's enough, Andrew. Here's a hundred dollars for your return fare. We'll flag the launch to take you to Beaufort. I shall expect to find that you are on the four-o'clock train home." That story was to show me how Red stood in Dad's household.

And it was the same with the crews at the Life Saving Station, where she was adopted and pampered by all the crewmen. Which turned out to be a wondrous thing.

The winter of 1912–13 was rough on shipping off Beaufort Inlet, just south of Cape Lookout. On October 20th, in early morning, a steamship flying the "I am on fire" flag was spotted by one of the surfmen. The motor lifeboat was launched, and

Dad and Red were part of the crew. Capt. Hart planned to beach his vessel, loaded with bales of cotton, ships stores and fruit. Mindful as always of the duty to save, if possible, not only passengers and crew but also cargo, Keeper Willis put his men to work fighting the fire which they did for sixty hours straight. All were saved in the case of the BERKSHIRE.

Dad would go on to tell me about the DORCHESTER, a steamer trying to salvage the ALCAZAR, which had been abandoned. And how, two days before Christmas, his crew started a pumping procedure that was to last into January. And about the THOMAS WINSMORE, a three-master, on which Dad and crew, with Red "assisting," hoisted anchors by hand and sailed into harbor.

But it was the wreck of the three-masted schooner, MANCHESTER HAYNES, on February 13, that makes this story. There was a SSW gale with very high seas. The captain could not clear the shoals, so anchored, but the deckload of yellow pine broke loose and she filled with water. The lifesaving crew was maneuvering to reach the disabled vessel, when the motor launch broached, throwing Red and six crewmen into the roaring surf. The Lookout shoals are sometimes shallow and sometimes deep. The winds from the SSW left some shoal water shallow enough so a man could stand—provided the undertow, or more properly the cross-currents, didn't sweep him out to sea. But between the shoals and the shore frequently lie deep sloughs. And humans wearing oilskins and sea boots, even if they kept their feet, had no hope of making land without help.

Somehow, my father said, Red seemed to sense the prospects, and the men's panic. She immediately swam to him and when he grabbed her collar, she headed straight northwest to shore. With that help, he fell flat on the sand, completely exhausted.

So he did not see, but only heard of, what happened next. Back went Red to her "boys" fighting to stay upright on the shoals. Three more times she ventured south into the wind to help a crewman back to safety. After four such rescues, the big, tough bitch would have tried again, but the last crewman, now on the beach, pulled her close. She never saw that two of the crew were no longer standing.

When Dad recovered enough strength to get upright, his first thought was for his dog. Down the beach he staggered until he came upon the survivors. Hugging Red to his chest, he wept for the lost members of the surfcrew. But those are the expected, those lost heroes of the Coast Guard. And for the Watermen and their dogs, life goes on.

Red continued to retrieve for Dad, and I, born two years later, remember her only as a tired old dog with a rusty coat and a grizzled muzzle. But on the little square in Chester there stands to this day a bronze marker, on which some sensitive sculptor of the Depression Federal Arts program has created a replica of a big Chesapeake looking out to sea. That's Red!

from DAVID HENDERSON'S DOG STORIES

Shep

NONA HENGEN

When I was a child, I read about a sheepdog that went down to the Great Northern Depot at Fort Benton, Montana, to meet every westbound train after the dog had watched the casket bearing its dead master's body being placed in a baggage car to be shipped east.

My recollections of this story came flooding back when a friend from Montana recently lent me a pamphlet that turned up among the private papers in her sister's estate: "Man's Best Friend—The Story of Shep, the Dog Who Was Ever Faithful," published by Ed Shields and Associates, and printed by the River Press in Fort Benton, Montana.

I sat down and read the story of this famous dog with renewed interest. It tells how, in August of 1936, a casket containing the body of a shepherd was placed on board a train in Fort Benton to be shipped east for burial. Unnoticed by those attending to this matter is a large collie-type dog watching workmen ease the casket onto the floor of a baggage car.

The train pulls slowly out of the station and disappears down the track. Every day for the next five years, the dog comes down out of the hills to meet the westbound train to see if his master is on board. When the last passenger steps down and his master isn't there, he retreats to await the arrival of the next train from the East. And the next train, and the next. He maintains this vigil for the rest of his life.

The pamphlet's author, Ed Shields, began his telling of the story with this dramatic opening statement: "Characterized as a nondescript sheepdog of pronounced collie strain, Shep became one of the most famous figures in all dogdom during his five-and-a-half-year vigil at the lonely Great Northern depot at Fort Benton, Montana . . . "

Shields was a conductor on one of the trains that passed through Fort Benton. He recognized the dog that turned up at the Fort Benton depot in August of 1936. He'd seen the dog before but hadn't assigned any significance to its presence until, he said, he had a casual conversation with a tracklayer stationed at Fort Benton, who rode the train 30 miles to his home in Virgelle on Saturday nights and returned on Monday mornings. One Monday morning when the train pulled into Fort Benton, Shields and the tracklayer stepped off the train together and there was the dog, looking at them expectantly. Shields asked the tracklayer who the dog belonged to. According to Shields, the tracklayer, who was "acquainted around there," gave this answer: "He belonged to a sheepherder that died. They shipped his body away and that dog has been hanging around here ever since."

Shields, who lived in Great Falls, made a few inquiries about the Fort Benton dog. He "called on several men, including Paul Louther, the undertaker, who has since passed away. That was the beginning of this story about Shep."

The original eight-page pamphlet, reprinted many times since 1939 when Great Northern published it to sell to passengers, gave rise to an oral tradition that grew up around Shields' presumption that a Montana shepherd had died in August of 1936, that his body was sent away for burial, and that his dog watched and waited for his return until five-and-a-half years later when, on January 12, 1942, the dog "failed to hear old 235" as it rolled into the station that wintry morning. The Fort Benton newspaper captioned a story two days later: "SHEP, FAMOUS FORT BENTON DOG, KILLED UNDER TRAIN ON MONDAY." And in smaller type, "Shep Attracted International Attention For Devotion To His Dead Sheepherder Master."

With his death, Shep's fame soared. The Associated Press and United Press International carried his obituary. The mayor of Great Falls was among the dignitaries attending Shep's grave-side service, conducted by the minister of Fort Benton's Christian Church. The Reverend Ralph Underwood spoke of Shep's faith-fulness unto death to his master. Boy Scout Troop 47 served as honor guard and pallbearers. Montana Senator George Graham Vest read the eulogy. Former Great Northern conductor, Ed Shields, who first brought the story of Shep's lonely vigil to light, was among the guests. As taps sounded, Shep's casket was low-ered into the ground on the windswept bluff overlooking the station, where he had waited so long for the return of his master.

Robert Ripley featured Shep in his famous "Believe It or Not" column in 1939; Paul Harvey featured Shep posthumously on February 19, 1988 in "The Rest of the Story."

A memorial service was held fifty years after Shep's death at the gravesite near the now-abandoned station, with words spoken by elderly men who remembered acting as pallbearers for Shep. Others of the same generation recalled those days when Shep haunted the depot platform waiting for trains to come in. A great deal of media attention followed in the wake of the 50th-year commemoration, including television coverage during the 1992 Westminster Dog Show held at Madison Square Garden.

Today, Shep's grave is maintained by the Fort Benton Community Improvement Association and the Kiwanis Club. There are no more passenger trains passing through Fort Benton, for now the railroad mostly carries grain. There is a Shep Memorial Fund to ensure the preservation of Shep's gravesite. Artist Bob Scriver, of Browning, Montana, 83 years old at the time, was present for the dedication of his heroic-size bronze statue of Shep, produced after a Shep look-alike contest was held and the winner taken to the artist's studio to pose for the "Shep— Forever Faithful" statue. The figure was installed in a beautiful, parklike setting along the Missouri River on Fort Benton's levee; it was unveiled and dedicated on June 26, 1994, with the artist present. Shep, already a tourist attraction, was thus immortalized in bronze.

The phenomenon of dogs meeting trains appears elsewhere in the annals of canine literature. Annie the Railroad Dog, whose story was told in the April, 1999 issue of *Dog & Kennel*, was a famous contemporary of Shep; she welcomed passengers stepping off the Colorado & Southern Railroad at the Fort Collins depot between 1934 and 1948. Like Shep, Annie was buried near the depot where she had spent most of her life. Bruno, of Bozeman, Montana, adopted Switch Engine No. 911 of the Northern Pacific and "followed it for seven years."

From the 1950s comes a fictionalized account of a dog that met trains bringing prisoners to a Soviet gulag during the Cold War era. Russian author Georgi Vladimov has written a moving dog story, which Michael Glenny translated and Simon &

Schuster published in 1978. *Faithful Ruslan* is an allegory about a dog used to guarding prisoners who, after the camps were dismantled in the late 1950s, continues his habit of going to the train station to meet the trains that formerly brought prisoners for him to guard.

Unlike Ruslan, Shep, Annie and Bruno were not fictional dogs. Yet one can examine certain parts of Shep's story, subject them to the rigors of historical analysis, and come up empty-handed. There are pieces in the mosaic of Shep's saga which remain unknown and perhaps, at this late date, unknowable; pieces missing, gaps bridged by oral tradition. Shep was real. His vigil, whether fact or myth, has become real to all those connected in some way to this famous dog.

Esther Tichenor, publisher of River Press in Fort Benton, provided copies of a number of memoirs forwarded by people familiar with Shep's era, and with Shep himself. When a Shep memorial and dedication project was undertaken, River Press invited people to submit first-person recall stories, and received a number of responses. One lady spoke of a childhood memory of her family driving to the depot to watch Shep meet the trains. Another remembered that the dining car stewards on trains No. 235 and No. 236 started to feed the dog steak—once in the morning, and once again in the evening, encouraging Shep's punctuality in meeting those trains. A woman told of sheep being gathered to cross the Old Bridge leading into town to move the flock to the corrals near the depot for shipping to summer pasture. Each shepherd had dogs; upon seeing this activity, "Shep came way down the hill" and volunteered to "help keep our little part of that band going in the right direction toward the corral." She added that Shep knew all the hand signals and every turn.

A man stated he was a member of the Boy Scout troop that carried Shep to his grave. Another recalled that the dog met each of the four passenger trains coming into Fort Benton every day. Yet another writer claimed the dog met passenger and freight trains alike, while a third claimed the dog might be inside the depot wandering around the platform when the trains arrived, but sometimes "he wasn't even there."

One man remembered that the manual training class at the local high school received the assignment of building Shep's casket. A woman, a senior in high school at the time, recorded an entry for January 14, 1942 in her diary: "I went with [a friend] to Shep's funeral. About 200 people were there . . . " Others living near the depot remembered their elders feeding the dog when he came to the house.

Bearing in mind that memory has a way of playing tricks, curiosity compelled me to search for primary source material—newspaper articles appearing in the late 1930s, mention of the dog in letters or diaries of the time, and the like. This led me to ask Nancy Compau, Northwest Room librarian of the Spokane Public Library, whether she had anything on file concerning this dog. She contacted Bob Clark, librarian of the Montana Historical Society at Helena on my behalf for information about Shep, and he responded to her inquiry with the following e-mail:

"The dog about which your patron inquires can be none other than Montana's Most Famous Dog, aka, Shep. Certain parts of the story are shaky enough to be legend already. That a shepherd had a family in the East that paid for his body to be shipped back is improbable enough, but that then no one, after just a couple of years, could come up with the name of the shepherd, or the date the alleged body was shipped out of a small town such as Fort Benton, well—but that's how the story goes.

"One would think that if there were a body it must have been embalmed at the one funeral parlor the town had, because memory puts the shipping in August, with the body already around for a few days, and if it wasn't embalmed one would think everyone would remember it at that time. So one would think there might have been a record that could be traced. But despite a lack of documentation surrounding the shepherd and the shipping, there clearly was a Shep, though that was just the name the [railway] station attached to the dog.

"In fact, there have been a few dissenters who have even said that Shep wasn't a particularly nice dog. Nevertheless, from 1936 until 1942, he did hang out at the Fort Benton railway depot and greeted trains, or showed some interest in them, to his eventual sorrow, as you shall see. In 1939, he gained national attention because he made it into Ripley's 'Believe It Or Not.' But what immortalized him, I think, was the ending, which was sad and dark, but somehow perfect. That is, he was run over by one of the trains that he was allegedly going out to meet to see if his master was on it. It doesn't get any better than that.

"He has now been written up in several magazines and booklets, he has a grave on a hill there in Fort Benton with a stone and monument, a statue and medallion by noted late Montana artist Bob Scriver, and he has to be considered one of Fort Benton's leading tourist attractions by any reasonable person.

"And you asked if we knew about that dog . . . "

Clark cited references to the Shep story as it appeared in

The Farm Journal of April, 1960, and also in the *Reader's Digest* of the same date. An updated version of the Shep story, "Forever Faithful," has been written by John G. and Sue Lepley, and was published by the River and Plains Society of Fort Benton in 1995. This booklet contains a "Facts of the Story" page where one learns that: first, Paul Louther, undertaker, accompanied Under Sheriff George Dickens in bringing the shepherd to the hospital, and also in sending his body to the East; second, a Sister Genevieve, Sister of Charity, at St. Claire Hospital, recalled feeding the dog at the back door during the days before the shepherd passed away; and third, station agent A.V. Schanche and section foreman Pat McSweeney were the ones who noticed the dog meeting the trains each day, and who "helped to compile the pieces that confirmed [Shep's] story."

Later compilations of Shep's story appear to rely on earlier versions, adding a detail here and there. None of these accounts mentions an examination of hospital records, funeral records or shipping records the depot might have kept that would be useful in discovering the identity of the shepherd, or at the very least, confirming his existence.

I asked the 83-year-old woman who lent me the original "Shep" pamphlet found among her late sister's papers how she would feel if part of Shep's story about keeping a vigil turned out to be a folktale. "I'd be very disappointed if it did," she replied simply.

Like my friend, I heard the story many years ago, was deeply touched by it, and had no reason to doubt it. When confronted with a rigorous dissection of the Shep story, the child in me feels disenchanted. The child in me savored the story of George Washington confessing to his father that he had indeed cut down a certain cherry tree and refused to lie about it when confronted. So, does it really matter whether the cherry tree—or the shepherd—existed? I think not.

Whether Shep's story is true, or a blend of fact and fiction, what matters most is the story is so dynamic that it is irresistible. We believe it because it speaks to something we hold to be generally true about dogs: That there are individuals among them who love us with unwavering devotion and with an intensity that carries the burden of loyalty to the grave and beyond.

from DOG & KENNEL

George L. Mountainlion

PAUL D. BUCHANAN

On November 5, 1953, a new column appeared in the *Arizona Daily Star*. Although the column itself was an unusual and interesting feature, it was the columnist that attracted the attention of Tucson, Arizona—for the columnist's name was George L. Mountainlion.

Actually, George had come to the Arizona-Sonora Desert Museum in February 1953 from California, where he was to share his enclosure with the then-resident mountain lion, Susie. Unable to get along with George, Susie was soon removed. But George stayed on, fascinating and charming more than 100,000 visitors to the museum each year.

In 1953, William H. Carr, a cofounder of the museum, was writing a column for the *Arizona Daily Star* called "Trailside Topics." One day the managing editor of the *Star*, Jack Weadock, commented on how attractive an animal George was, and how something special should be done in the column to highlight him. It was suggested that the readers might be interested in a column from the mountain lion's point of view. The editor readily agreed, and on November 5, 1953, the column had a new by-line. From that point on, "Trailside Topics by George L. Mountainlion" appeared in the Sunday *Arizona Daily Star*, with several ghostwriters contributing over the years.

The column featured stories about the animals of the Arizona-Sonora Desert Museum. This museum (founded in 1952), located ten miles west of Tucson, was established in 1955 as an independent community educational institution. Its purpose is to provide information on the desert life surrounding the Tucson area. It features displays of large and small species of the Sonora Desert, a desert garden, a walk-in aviary, the Beaver-Otter-Bighorn Sheep Complex, and the Congdon Earth Sciences Center, highlighting underground cave life and geology. And, of course, the main attraction over the years has been its mountain lion.

Actually, mountain lions—*Puma concolor,* also known as pumas, cougars, catamounts, and other monikers—rarely make it as Sunday newspaper columnists. As the only large cat indigenous to the United States, the mountain lion is often regarded as the most magnificent animal in the country. Unfortunately, it has also achieved a reputation as a dangerous animal, although attacks upon humans are extremely rare. Spontaneous attacks occur most often during times of extended drought, when the cat's usual prey—anything from deer to rabbits and raccoons—moves closer to water sources, which are often close to human developments. Normally, mountain lions are shy, secretive animals, which is why human attempts to study the beast have revealed relatively little.

The range of the mountain lion—in Arizona or anywhere in the United States—is often a matter for extensive speculation. The big cat no doubt inhabits expansive territory in Arizona, where much of the land is untouched by humans. But again, because of the species' inconspicuous habits, mapping the habitats of mountain lions can be a frustrating and even futile endeavor.

Over the years—particularly in the late nineteenth to early twentieth century—ranchers saw mountain lions as threats to livestock, and efforts to exterminate them grew to nearly maniacal levels. No doubt cougars have taken their share of domestic cattle and sheep over the decades, particularly during those times of drought when natural prey is less accessible. But normally the potential food supply for a mountain lion is so great, and the big cat's skill as a hunter is so sharp, that it will avoid the great hazard of raiding domestic stocks and exposing itself to human encounters. When mountain lions and people cross paths, it is normally because people have invaded the cat's territory, and not the other way around.

Partly due to the quality of the writing, and partly due to the public's fascination with *Puma concolor,* the response to George L. Mountainlion's column was overwhelming. Mail poured in. Many of the readers were children, and their letters were often addressed simply "George, Tucson, Arizona." Letters also came from adults, not only from Tucson and throughout Arizona, but from surrounding states as well.

Although the column ran in the *Arizona Daily Star* for 16 years, the original George L. Mountainlion died on March 8, 1955. George the First was buried on the museum grounds, with a handsome marble headstone commemorating him. His epitaph reads as follows:

> *I freely give all sights and sounds of nature I have known to those who have the grace to enjoy not man-made materialism but God-made beauty.*
> *The magnificent Arizona sunsets I have watched from my enclosure, I bequeath to all who see not only with their eyes but with their hearts.*

To humans who are tired, worried or discouraged, I bequeath the silence, majesty, and peace of our great American desert.

To those who walk the trails, I bequeath the early morning voices of the birds, and the glory of the flowering desert in the springtime.

To the children who have enjoyed seeing me, hearing me purr, and watching me turn my somersaults, I offer the precious gift of laughter and joy. The world so needs these things.

And lastly, I bequeath my own happy spirit, and affection for others, to all who may remember me and my museum where for three years, I did my best to show people that I truly liked them.

from FAMOUS ANIMALS OF THE STATES

ACKNOWLEDGMENTS
(continued from page ii)

"A Cat on Tour" is from *A Cat Abroad,* by Peter Gethers. Copyright © 1993 by Peter Gethers. Published by Ballantine Books.

"Rin Tin Tin," "Tom, Tony and Duke" and "A Picture-Perfect Cow" are from *Not So Dumb,* by Raymond Lee. © 1970 by A. S. Barnes and Co., Inc. Published by A. S. Barnes and Co., Inc.

"Scruffy in the Spotlight" is from *Super Animals and Their Unusual Careers,* by Virginia Phelps Clemens. Copyright © 1979 Virginia Phelps Clemens. Published by The Westminster Press.

"A President's Pup" is from *First Dogs,* by Roy Rowan and Brooke Janis. © 1997 by Roy Rowan and Brooke Janis. Published by Algonquin Books of Chapel Hill, a division of Workman Publishing.

"The World's Most-Traveled Dog," by Leila Dornak, is from *Our Best Friends,* by Michael Capuzzo and Teresa Banik Capuzzo. Copyright © 1998 by Michael Capuzzo and Teresa Banik Capuzzo. Published by Bantam Books.

"The Changing Seasons" is from *My Dog Skip,* by Willie Morris. © 1995 Willie Morris. Published by Random House, Inc.

"The Wisest One" is from *The Story of Scotch,* by Enos Mills. Copyright 1909, 1911 and 1916 by Enos Mills. Published by Alpine Publications.

"Devotion" is from *Hero Dogs,* by Peter C. Jones and Lisa MacDonald. Copyright © 1997 by Peter C. Jones and Lisa MacDonald. Published by Andrews and McMeel.

"Red Dog Retriever" is from *David Henderson's Dog Stories.* Copyright © 1998 by David H. Henderson and Shepard H. Foley. Published by Winchester Press, an imprint of New Win Publishing, Inc.

"Shep," by Nona Hengen, is from *Dog & Kennel,* October 1999.

A Note From
the Editors

This original Guideposts series was created by the Book and Inspirational Media Division of the company that publishes *Guideposts,* a monthly magazine filled with true stories of people's adventures in faith. *Guideposts* is available by subscription. All you have to do is write to Guideposts, 39 Seminary Hill Road, Carmel, New York 10512. When you subscribe, each month you can count on receiving exciting new evidence of God's presence, His guidance and His limitless love for all of us.

Guideposts is also available on the Internet by accessing our home page on the World Wide Web at www.guideposts.org. Send prayer requests to our Monday morning Prayer Fellowship. Read stories from recent issues of our magazines, *Guideposts, Angels on Earth, Clarity, Guideposts for Kids* and *Guideposts for Teens,* and follow our popular book of daily devotionals, *Daily Guideposts.* Excerpts from some of our best-selling books are also available.